The Vegetarian's Self-defense Manual

Cover art by *Jane A Evans*

The Vegetarian's

Self-defense Manual

By

RICHARD BARGEN, M.D.

is publication made possible with the assistance of the Kern Foundation

THE THEOSOPHICAL PUBLISHING HOUSE
Wheaton, Ill. U.S.A./Madras, India/London, England

A Quest original, published by the Theosophical
Publishing House, a department of the Theosophical Society in America. Inquiries for permission to
reproduce all, or portions of this book should be
addressed to Quest Books, 306 West Geneva Road,
Wheaton, Illinois 60187.

Library of Congress Cataloging in Publication Data

Bargen, Richard, 1946-
    The vegetarian's self-defense manual.

    Bibliography: p.
    1. Vegetarianism. I. Title
RM236.B34   613.2'6   79-64097
ISBN 0-8356-0530-2 pbk.

PREFACE

This first compendium of all the major scientific studies concerned with vegetarianism should be of interest and benefit to both lay persons and professionals alike. Changes in "official" thinking on nutrition are just around the corner and as the world moves towards the adoption of an adequate vegetarian diet, as the standard in nutrition, it becomes extremely important that the scientific basis of this diet is firmly established by research and study.

The research done thus far is only a beginning. While one hopes that it would, like holding the cross before a vampire, dispel many of the misconceptions and fables about vegetarianism, it is obvious from a scientific point of view that a more comprehensive "cross" is yet required.

Nonetheless, the reader will find much valuable information reviewed in this book, hopefully in a readable fashion. The professional reader, especially one unfamiliar with or uneasy with vegetarians, will gain an appreciation of the scientific basis underlying the functioning of these strange creatures. "Be not afraid of vegetariansim: Some are born vegetarian, some achieve vegetarianism, and some have vegetarianism thrust upon them." (with apologies to William Shakespeare)

I thank my editor, Rosemarie Stewart, for her help in the preparation of the manuscript. To my wife, Heather, who aided greatly in the collection of all this material, a special thanks.

RICHARD BARGEN, M.D.

CONTENTS

1

IS THERE LIFE
AFTER VEGETARIANISM?

Roots—Definition of Terms

A carpet of wild grasses stretched in the dim, golden twilight to a secret horizon; the faint musical cries of the night-birds heralded the appearance of the full moon above the rolling hills. Quietly, the warm evening winds began their sweep up the great river, carressing the small groves of flatland poplar and occasional, solitary white birch. Rising from the deep, shadow-filled valleys, the crests of the tallest hills, basking peacefully in the fading evenlight, were seen to be sprinkled with scattered herds of Hereford cattle which grazed slowly downwind, filling their bellies with succulent prairie grasses. At first enchanting glance I thought, "what a delightful scene!" Yet, inevitably, a disquietening, vague feeling, a metaphysical 'angst' arose in my vegetarian heart as I pondered the reality of the view spread out before me, that is that the ultimate fate of these quadrupeds was a not so peaceful journey to a human's dinner table! The thought distressed me. The dimming western light issued one last challenge to the coming of the night, a small purple flare lingered hopefully but then vanished as a torrent of black shadows rushed across the land lying silent beneath the restless night sky.

The truck's headlights picked out the winding trail home. ('No, Virginia, as a rule vegetarians can't see in the dark'). Thoughts of vegetarianism and its proposed takeover of the world were again tempered by the aforementioned realities. In North America and several other parts of the world, flesh foods are a giant industry. Many humans enjoy hunting animals, enjoy eating meat, and see no reason to change their habits. Often those who would open-mindedly consider some sort of dietary changes, adopting vegetarianism, are frightened away by various widespread myths and misconceptions about the problems encountered on the road to becoming a skinny, anemic herbivore. "What about protein? I know I can't live without protein!" What about vitamin B_{12}?" "What about...", if you now see what I mean. Can there possibly be life after vegetarianism?

Having become a vegetarian for purely philosophical reasons, simply viewing the consumption of food as an interruption of the day's activities, a necessary evil perhaps (perhaps also a slight exaggeration), this writer confesses that it was the questions noted above plus the concern of family, regarding a possible early demise—"The grave's a fine and private place, But none I think do there embrace"—that first prompted my excursions into the scientific literature on vegetarianism. I sought to glean a few facts with which to assure others that, (1) death was not imminent; (2) lack of vitamin B_{12} would not destroy my nervous system five years hence; and that (3) *good heavens!*, there was even hope that I might maintain some semblance of good health.

The reader would be rapidly persuaded, even upon cursory examination of the popular literature on nutrition (and often, unfortunately, the 'scientific' literature), that in no field of human concern, save perhaps religion, are such widely and wildly varying opinions held—and as noisily advanced—frequently bereft of any rational or scientific underpinnings. The sun of enlightenment had as yet not risen over the literary landscape which I was exploring. Proponents of every conceivable dietary persuasion claimed, with absolute conviction, that the sole path to health and nutritional salvation led only through the particular dietary territory which they had staked out for themselves.

Little imagination is needed to see what effect this sort of thing might have upon one who had learned to appreciate the methodology of scientific inquiry; it became a question of survival, both intellectual and physical. Where was all the material that supposedly existed, dealing with vegetarianism and the scientific foundations if any upon which it stands? Subsequently, searches of the literature unearthed isolated, sporadic studies, anecdotal information and a fair amount of unsubstantiated speculation. But, disappointingly, nothing of a systematic nature and certainly nothing resembling a compendium of useful scientific information on vegetarians was unearthed. It was clear that no one in recent years had found this void objectionable enough to instigate a project to correct it (to separate the chaff from the meat, so to speak). You will now undoubtedly understand why one who would prefer existence without the burden of an alimentary tract, should have so fearlessly undertaken the following resolve; that is to gather together between two covers all the major scientific literature (English language), on human vegetarians both for selfish interests and for the amusement of those persons, lay or professional, who would find the accumulation of this information a benefit. Much of the information reviewed in the following chapters should be of great interest to the lay vegetarian, both to provide some scientific substantiation for a still frequently assailed lifestyle and also to remove any doubts or anxieties he or she may feel about the diet's nutritional adequacies. The main body of the book is written at a lay level so that, "A child of five would understand this. Send somebody to fetch a child of five."

Medical professionals unfamiliar and uneasy with vegetarian patients will also find the book helpful. It is written at lay level, yet the research papers compiled in the bibliography are unique and comprehensive, and the reviews in the appropriate chapters touch on all the pertinent medical points.

An interesting future project would be a book on the scientific nutrition of vegetarians, discussing the various foods available, their food values etc. Hopefully, the present effort, to simply collect the scientific research, presently available, dealing with vegetarians, will be a step in the right direction. (If this book is successful I'm sure you'll find the subsequent film adaptation even more entertaining. Robert Redford is negotiating for the part of Vitamin B_{12} and appears quite interested—providing the celery is right).

The reader will encounter several preparatory chapters. The section on the scientific method was included specifically for the benefit of vegetarian lay persons, who in Western countries at least, tend to adopt (for various reasons) what might be described as anti-scientific attitudes, mistakenly so I believe. It would be nice if, after reading through that short chapter, a reader such as described above, would realize what a close affinity science (true science), and 'the search for truth' really have.

For the newcomer, the chapter on the history of vegetarianism should provide background information helpful to understanding this magnificent creed and demonstrate how long and successfully this aberrant dietary has played upon the stage of human nourishment.

In order to ensure that we will be comparing oranges with oranges and apples with apples, the following paragraphs define some pertinent terminology. While it would seem rudimentary to have everyone agree upon the meaning of the important terms we'll be using, the ever-present problem of facilitating communication is often somewhat intransigent. A recent illustration is provided by a paper (Fall of 1978) in the *New England Journal of Medicine*, one of my favorite journals, in which the terms 'vegan', 'strict vegetarian' and 'vegetarian' were used *interchangeably* by the authors. The result was that false deductions were made and great consternation was stirred up in those readers who were familiar with the terms and realized, as you also will shortly, that they describe different types of creatures.

To characterize the human herbivore clearly, it's been found helpful to designate several sub-species, which follow. But first let me surprise many readers with the proper definition of a basic term...'vegetarian'. It was in 1842 that we first note the use of the word 'vegetarian'. While it is commonly thought that the word refers to eaters-of-vegetables, this is not the case, as the linguistic derivation stems from the Latin *vegetus*, meaning "whole, sound, fresh, and lively." The Latin term for vegetable is *vegetabilus*; thus many vegetarians may also be vegetabilarians but all vegetabilarians need not necessarily be vegetarians; the latter word implies the adoption of a life-style designed to harmonize one with the 'cosmic forces'. However, you will find the word 'vegetarian' often used in this book in the commonly accepted way, i.e., referring to the dietary practice of not allowing flesh foods. Purists, of course, will delight in using these terms properly, exulting in that special feeling which arises when only you and perhaps one other person on earth have any idea of what you are talking about.

Let's clarify a few more concepts. First, to define the noble vegan, we can do no better than to quote from the definition provided by the Vegan Society itself:

> Veganism is a way of living which excludes all forms of exploitation of, and cruelty to, the animal kingdom, and includes a reverence and compassion for all life. It applies to the practice of living on the products of the plant kingdom to the exclusion of flesh, fish, fowl, eggs, honey, animal milk, and its derivatives, and encourages the use of alternatives for all commodities derived wholly or in part from animals. Veganism remembers man's responsibilities to the earth....

Vegetarian, what a fine sounding word; it just rolls melodiously off the tongue. There are several sub-types of vegetarians:

a. Lacto-vegetarian: a vegan who does consume such animal products as milk and cheese. These animal products do not kill the animal. Some loss of purity is entailed. (The writer's dietary persuasions fall under this heading).

b. Lacto-ovo-vegetarian: self-explanatory, no examples (egg-samples?), needed.

c. Temporary vegetarian: a good-willed experimenter who will subsist on potatoes and cabbage for periods of up to one month before regretfully deciding that the vegetarian lifestyle is not a viable alternative for the civilized human being.

d. Miscellaneous: These are usually self-explanatory variations such as fruitarians, nutarians, etc. The Macrobiotic diet (to be discussed later) is only vegetarian when the higher numbered diets are attained. If any of the readers should find themselves and their whole approach to life listed here under 'miscellaneous', please don't be insulted. Some of my best friends fall into this category; many people feel that a distinct advantage in life and karma is possessed by those who attain a 'miscellaneous' classification. For example, there are some vegans who insist that their strictly plant diets should be eaten raw only.

Finally, there are two other definitions which the reader may find helpful:

1. Eaters-of-flesh: Also known as 'meat-eaters' or carnivores. Surprisingly, to the Westerner at least, on the

global scale of dietaries, these humans form a minority, though in North America they constitute the majority. These beings feed off the carcasses of a variety of their fellow creatures (cannibalism being a variant much frowned upon in higher circles), all of whom have been especially killed and prepared for this 'sub-species' dining delight. Muscle fibre, fats and internal organs, after suitable processing by specialists, are consumed, often to such an extent, that dead animals may constitute 50% or more of the person's dietary intake. A majority of these people must have their flesh foods cooked, chopped up, or essentially disguised in various fashions in order to consume them without some feelings of revulsion. Perhaps we should consider them to be 'latent vegetarians'. It is important to realize that in the literature, those who fall into this category are considered to be the 'norm'; thus we find studies comparing the vegetarian diet with the 'normal' diet. Consequently much of the scientific literature on nutrition and most studies in human physiology are actually based exclusively on data collected from this one group of human beings, with important implications which will be expanded upon in later chapters.

2. The literature: In science, reviewing 'the literature' in a particular field, refers to the process of researching through all the accepted sources of scientific information on a certain subject, in our case vegetarianism. 'Literature' consists mainly of articles in various scientific journals which are generally published several times yearly. All scientific literature is indexed under appropriate headings in several massive, continuously up-dated volumes which have now been augmented by computerized accessing. The references collected and reviewed in this book are available, for the most part, in any large university associated library. Thus with the help of the bibliography at the end of the book the reader should have easy access to any of the papers in which he or she is interested simply by personally writing to or visiting a major library.

Just what are these indexed sources? The six most comprehensive sources of information used in preparing this book are listed below:

a. Index Medicus
b. Surgeon-General's Office Index
c. Biological Abstracts
d. Nutrition Reviews and Abstracts
e. Med-Line Computer Indexing
f. Additional references supplied by each author at the end of each published paper

To reiterate, it is hoped that this book will be of service to two, supposedly disparate, groups of readers; first, vegetarians who are interested in determining what is known of the scientific basis for their diet, and second, those who deal with the increasing numbers of vegetarians in a professional capacity (physicians and others) and require a source of information and references on this subject. Again, this is not a treatise on nutrition. The author, due to limits imposed by lifespan, has not pursued the subject to the same extent as did one writer in 1846, who entitled his work: "On abstinence from the flesh of animals as food; introductory to a consideration of the subject in relation to the habitual reasoning of men, popular opinion, domestic economy, and the facts of chemistry, anatomy, physiology, history, morality and religion."

The author also hopes that attempts at 'light-hearted' writing in this book are not construed by the reader as indications that the subject matter is not considered to be of great importance to mankind in general, but rather a display of his personal brand of humor.

Who's Who

Every minority group being persecuted by the general population will take heart when they hear of a few famous and generally respected persons who agree with its minority views. Thus, what follows may be used by the disheartened for a little chin-upping; to be sure, a few villains have been vegetarians but I'm sure no one is anxious to hear about them.

Certainly one of the all-time greats and an acknowledged giant in His field, God, is a vegetarian. This undeniable conclusion is drawn from His famous, best-selling reference work, the Bible, wherein He is quoted instructing embryonic humanity:

I give you all the seed-bearing plants that are upon the whole earth, and all the trees with seed-bearing fruit; this shall be your food.

(Genesis 1:29)

Regrettably, the promise of the early creation became clouded, and as the darker aspects of the human creature emerged, with the resultant devastation of the Flood, God apparently allowed some flesh foods. He did stipulate that no foods containing blood were to be eaten. (Genesis 9:3)

Somewhat later, prompted by Man's hopes for the future and the approaching Messianic Age, Isaiah scanned the temporal horizon with his prophetic eye and reported to us what lay ahead. He describes the coming events in picturesque language.

"The wolf lives with the lamb,
the panther lies down with the kid,
calf and lion cub feed together
with a little boy to lead them.
The cow and the bear make friends,
their young lie down together.
The lion eats straw like the ox.
The infant plays over the cobra's hole;
into the viper's lair the young child puts his hand.
They do no hurt, no harm,
on all my holy mountain,
for the country is filled with
the knowledge of Yahweh
as the water swells the sea."

(Isaiah 11:6-9)

Now, if this poem describes conditions in the anticipated Messianic Age, and if every Christian prays, with any earnestness at all, "Let Thy Kingdom come on earth,..." then it follows, as surely as night the day, that all Christians would taste something of that future bliss by adopting a vegetarian lifestyle without delay. St. Paul certainly agreed (for his own theological reasons), stating:

That is why, since food can be the occasion of my brother's downfall, I shall never eat meat again in case I am the cause of a brother's downfall.

(1 Cor. 8:13, New Jerusalem Bible)

It appears to me that if He sees 'the little sparrow fall', it is not inconceivable that He would be distressed by the continuing unnecessary slaughter and consumption of millions of His sentient creatures.

Through the ages, the Magis, Hindus, Buddhists, Jains, the Sufis, and many other religious groups have advocated the vegetarian diet. "A fleshless diet has been, from time immemorial, the recommended dietary for those seeking spiritual advancement".

Pythagorus, an amazing historical figure, lived in the sixth century B.C. He both advocated and masticated a vegetarian dietary. Plato notes in his *Republic* that although lesser societies might not be expected to follow a plant food diet alone, the ideal society which he was proposing could and would be confirmed vegetarians. Empedocles, Plutarch, Porphyry, Pliny, Horace, Ovid, and Virgil all recommended a fleshless diet. Clement of Alexandria, a prominent 'Father of the Church', exhorted the Church to abstain from the flesh of animals, as there were more than enough products of an herbivorous nature available to sustain healthful living. Around 800 A.D. the Rule of St. Benedict enforced the fleshless dietary for monks; the diet of present-day Trappist Monks is a direct descendent of this earlier formulation.

In all walks of life we find devotees of the fleshless diets. Shakespeare and Bacon appear to have been sympathetic to vegetarianism. A small sample from the vegetarian grab-bag includes Milton, Pope, Voltaire, Rousseau, Thoreau, Linneaus, Wesley, Tolstoy, the Captain and Tennille, Issac Newton, Shelley, Gandhi, George Bernard Shaw, the Theosophists, the Doukhobors and, if the *Encyclopedia Britannica* is to be believed, the Salvation Army. The list of well-known vegetarians seems endless. Just as significantly, of course, many of us unknowns cling fanatically to this sublime dietary habit, never gracing the pages of history with our names, yet quietly munching and crunching along our way, while the trackless sands of time flow ceaselessly onwards, our only prayer being, "Deliver us Herbivorous."

Institutionally, in Western countries at least, the vegetarian diet has a fairly distinct history. In 1809 the vegetarian 'Bible Christian Church' was founded in England. Not too many years later, a number of devotees sailed for North America and a new life (reports of some backsliding on the long journey must surely be in error). Sylvester Graham, renowned creator of the

Graham Cracker, was a confessed vegetarian. During the mid-eighteen hundreds the Seventh Day Adventists were born and, for the most part, advocated vegetarianism as a way of life. The Kellogg brothers were involved with the Seventh Day Adventists and made their fortunes remedying the ailments in the North American diet. A most readable (though not reverent) account of this era is found in the book *Cornflake Crusade* by Carson.

Earlier we had mentioned the first use of the word 'vegetarian' (in approximately 1842). In 1847 the first independent 'Vegetarian Society' came into being, again the English taking the lead. Vegetarian societies rapidly became the rage, spreading out to the far corners of the world within a few short years. Many such societies thrive today and interested readers will have no difficulty making contact with a group. Periodically, on the global scale, International Vegetarian Conferences are held.

In 1889, 7,000 lacto-ovo-vegetarian Doukhobors immigrated to Western Canada, certainly enlarging the vegetarian population of this portion of the country considerably. Those days, toward the end of the nineteenth century, heralded the onset of what might be considered primitive 'scientific literature' on the subject of vegetarianism. However, it should be remarked that even in comparison with other fields of scientific interest, the science of nutrition was exceedingly long on art and short on science and really remained so for the first few decades of our present century. An investigator named Hardinge (of whom you will hear more later) writes:

> The earlier scientific literature is limited mainly to discussions of comparative anatomy and to medical reasoning based on observation of the effects of various diets on the well-being of the consumers. Little more could be done until the scientific knowledge necessary for nutritional research as we know it today was sufficiently developed.

By now the sensitive reader will have perceived that the plot is thickening and the book is building to a climax. However, you should restrain yourself while we consider another important preliminary—that is, an explanation of the common reasons advanced for adopting the vegetarian diet (the *etiology* of vegetarianism, so to speak).

Etiology [Eatiology?]

Item: a recent major food commission study in Norway recommended that the country's government institute such food policies that would result in decreased consumption of meat and in increased consumption of plant foods for, amongst other important reasons, the relationships of meat-eating and major cardiovascular disease were to be so closely intertwined ("...like finding a trout in the milk"). A male aged 40 years had a greater chance of reaching 70 years in 1900 than he does today. Surprisingly, perhaps, most of the world's population is in reality vegetarian (using the term colloquially); however, the quality of the diets in use range from the banquet class to the heart-breaking level. Inhabitants of the developing countries are plant eaters mainly of necessity, the choice of foods often exceedingly limited and the quantities markedly restricted. We, in the 'developed countries', usually have a significant degree of freedom in choosing the plant foods for our diets, yet the trend is increasing for the governments of most Western nations to recommend less food from animal sources and more dietary plant products.

Etiology is the study of 'causes'. The 'cause' of vegetarianism is multi-faceted. It would be very pleasing to be able to present clearcut evidence that the natural inclination of the human species is toward a plant food diet, but all I have to offer is anecdotal evidence at present. The extent to which our dietary preferences are conditioned by habit and culture requires little further comment. It is a common finding that infants do often require time to acquire a taste for meat, not infrequently rejecting this food to begin with. We are now talking about our Western society. In predominantly vegetarian India, it would be rare for a person to switch to meat-eating simply because the flesh is available. Personally, this writer has had two patients, one a 7-year-old boy and the other an eight-year-old boy, brought for medical attention by their respective mothers for the sole reason that they had, since birth, refused to eat meat or eggs. Both were healthy, active children in whom no sign of disease or malnutrition could be found. They were presented to me over a year apart, were not related, and came from strongly meat-eating families deep in the heart of ranching country. Some writers have stated that the fact that man never rushes out after killing an animal and rips into it for a raw meal, indicates a difference between him and the carnivores. Perhaps so. Archeology presents evidence that man has long used animals for food, but this is the Aquarian Age and things have changed for the better. We no longer need to go second class.

So, what is the etiology of vegetarianism? Popular and scientific articles conclude that there are four basic reasons that people adhere to this heavenly dietary. The vast majority of vegetarians will probably find themselves categorized under one of the four headings below:

1. *Cultural* reasons—very powerful influences on what one eats, what one considers good, and what one avoids as food or, to paraphrase Spiro, "One group chews what another group eschews."

    Religious beliefs are very important in determining a person's dietary persuasions. Vegetarianism is, and has always been, considered to have a strong influence on spiritual aspirations and attainments. Daniel, of the lion's den fame, found the diet most conducive to his survival. Religious ideals are often closely intertwined with the 'ethical' aspects of the diet, discussed below.

2. *Health*—the popular literature on vegetarianism is filled with statements assuring us that this fare will help us live longer, remain healthier, work better, think better, and have greater physical endurance. The scientific credentials for such statements are usually unimpressive (thus far, at least), except perhaps for the latter category. There is a good deal of documented evidence that vegetarians do better than average in events that require a great deal of physical endurance. Vegetarians also like to think that they are healthier than average because of the diet and I agree. During my recent bout of hepatitis, for example, while most people would have been deathly ill, I was only sick as a dog, and this can only have been due to the protective effects of the vegetarian diet. (My wife commented that my wonderfully yellow eyes, which glowed even in the dark, were symbols of vitality.) Historically, that diet and disease are closely intertwined cannot be denied:

Whatsoever was the father of a disease, an ill diet was the mother.

(Old proverb)

The fact remains that many of the world's 'long-livers' such as the Hunzas, live on substantially vegetarian fare. Whether their good health derives from the type of food or from their generally lower calorie intake, or both, is still not clear. Much more may be said but let's conclude with a quote from someone who should know, Percy Bysshe Shelley:

There is no disease, bodily or mental, which the adoption of vegetable diet and pure water has not infallibly mitigated, wherever the experiment has been fairly tried.

3. *Economic*—those who are vegetarian for primarily economic reasons, fall into two categories. The first aspect involves poverty, meaning that when poor, one buys the cheapest foods available, and this invariably predicates local plant food over flesh food. It also restricts one to perhaps a single type of plant food, which can lead to problems.

Rich people seldom are hungry.
Malnutrition and Poverty
(John Hopkins University Press)

After having spent several years overseas in the 'less developed nations', this writer has yet to see an exception to the above statement.

"Feeding food"—this is the second aspect of this heading. Food also needs to be fed and the reader will have no difficulty finding reams of data which demonstrate the great economy of living on plant foods, as opposed to flesh foods. In general terms, the production of plant food per unit of land is usually more than 10 times that achieved when the plant food is cycled through animals prior to consumption. The sun being the primary source of energy for our solar system, many vegetarians feel that living on this diet enables them to live lower on the food chain and closer to this essential energy source. The ecosphere finds the vegetarian much

easier to support. Many find the economic reasons for becoming vegetarian, quite persuasive.

An earlier predictive and engaging paper scripted by Hall in 1911, reviewed vegetarianism from an omnivore's point of view. He states:

> Although as yet only a matter of speculative interest possessed of no argumentative value, there is another aspect of the vegetarian diet worth consideration, and that is the greater economy and consequent inevitableness as soon as the world's population grows up to the limit of the land available for cultivation. All flesh is grass...

Greater detail on this subject may be found in two interesting works of recent origin; the first, 'Food: Politics, Economics, Nutrition and Research', was compiled by the American Association for the Advancement of Science and was edited by Abelson. The second is the September 1976 issue of *Scientific American* which devoted the entire issue to food and agriculture. Lettuce close with one quote from the latter:

> The annual production of fixed carbon by green plants on land and in the seas is about 150 billion tons; human consumption is about 260 pounds per person. Thus the energy captured by plants far exceeds human needs; if it could all be directed to human nutrition, it could support a population of 1.15 trillion, more than 280 times the present population. The food supply is not limited by a scarcity of sunshine.

4. *Ethical* considerations—one of the best spokesmen for the diet said:

> Like many of my contemporaries, I had rarely for many years used animal food, or tea, or coffee, etc.; not so much because of any ill effects which I had traced to them, as because they were not agreeable to my imagination. The repugnance to animal food is not the effect of experience, but is an instinct. It appeared more beautiful to live low and fare hard in many respects; and though I never did so, I went far enough to please my imagination. I believe that every man who has ever been earnest to preserve his higher or poetic faculties in the best condition has been particu-

larly inclined to abstain from animal food, and from much food of any kind.... Whatever my own practice may be, I have no doubt that it is a part of the destiny of the human race, in its gradual improvement, to leave off eating animals, as surely as the savage tribes have left off eating each other when they came in contact with the more civilized.

(Henry David Thoreau, *Walden*)

The ethical attractions of the vegetarian habit are really unassailable and to this writer constitute the most powerful and compelling arguments in its favor. Some of the ethical aspects of this question may even be open to scientific verification. For example, man generally has not as yet become aware of the consciousness existing in the higher animals but increasingly the mental processes of animals are being explored by scientists and will, I'm sure, eventually convince many, that animals do have consciousness and that eating them is "uncivilized". A recent offering on this subject is "The Question of Animal Awareness—Evolutionary Continuity of Mental Experience" (Rockefeller Univ. Press, 1976).

Much of the older literature on vegetarian diet is devoted to endless arguments on this particular question. The acknowledged classic in this field is by Williams. His 19th century contemporary, Salt, covers most of the arguments against vegetarianism, including ethical considerations, in an entertaining paper from which we will draw our closing quotation:

But are there not other reasons alleged against the practice of vegetarianism? Ah, those dear old Fallacies, so immemorial yet ever new, how can I speak disrespectfully of what has so often refreshed and entertained me! Every food-reformer is familiar with them—the 'law of nature' argument, which would approximate human ethics to the standard of the tiger-cat or rattle-snake; the 'necessity-of-taking-life' argument, which conscientiously ignores the question of unnecessary killing; the 'blubber' argument, or to put it more exactly, the 'what would become of the Eskimo?' to which the only answer is, a system of state-aided emigration; the 'for my sake' argument, which may be called the family fallacy; the 'what should we do without leather?' that lurid picture of a shoeless world instantaneously converted to vegetarianism; and the disinterested 'what would become of the animals' argument, which foresees the grievous wanderings of homeless herds who can find no kind protector to eat them. Best of all, I think, is what may be termed the metaphysical argument, beloved of learned men, which urges that it is better for the animals to live and be eaten than not to live at all—an imaginary ante-natal choice in an imaginary antenatal condition!

Perhaps other important 'causes' of vegetarianism exist, but most vegetarians will undoubtedly find that one or the other of the aforementioned headings was the most influential in their adoption or continued adherence to the diet.

The core of this book, the review of the various scientific studies on vegetarianism lies just ahead. Making this large body of scientific information entertaining, is not an easy task, but if the inquiring reader will bring enough persistence to the task of reviewing the data, then when he or she is done, they will be filled with pride and new understanding in this inimitable way of life. And on the day, when you finish this tome, you will say (along with John Lennon): "It was something special, a day amongst days...a red lettuce day".

Science and Vegetarianism
[for the 'new vegetarians']

It is impossible to explain 'science' in one short chapter, perhaps because it means so many things to so many different people. However, with the help of quotes from a number of eminent scientists and a few of this writer's impressions, I hope that those readers who belong to the "new vegetarians" (to whom this section is addressed), the large group of contemporary "Western" vegetarians so distrustful of 'scientists', will find that true science is really an equivalent to religious searching, but involved with the 'material' world, utilizing an agreed upon set of rules of conduct as a 'guide' in order to avoid serious error.

There are many ways to knowledge—faith, experience, science, etc. Science is limited. Science deals with the material universe. It begins with observation of objects or events, and these events may also be results of experiments. From the observations one obtains measurements and data. The data are used to form generalizations and from these generalizations spring hypotheses about events or objects as yet unobserved. The next step is the testing of the hypothesis by experiment, gathering more data, etc. As a result, the hypothesis may be abandoned as it simply doesn't explain new information. Or it may be confirmed completely, which might result in a theory being formed about the subject of interest. Scientists should be able to confirm the results of experiments independently of each other. The reader can see from this simple explanation that the process of science, in a sense, parallels the way people often think normally, but simply is more rigorous in its approach.

It is only in the last few hundred years that the development and practical application of the scientific method has begun to take over from unsubstantiated dogmatism or speculation, although it appears that certain forms of thinking we might consider "unscientific", are making a comeback. The roots of "science" are set deep within the human soul.

> What science has to teach us here is not its techniques but its spirit; the irresistible need to explore.
>
> —Bronowski

> Facts are not science—as the dictionary is not literature.
>
> —Martin Fischer

Theories and hypotheses come and go, yet the approach remains, and the spirit of the search makes of every person a scientist.

> "Men love to wonder and that is the seed of our Science"
>
> —Emerson

Of course, a few persons of "stature" have other thoughts on what "science" is all about. George Bernard Shaw and Mark Twain explain some of the main objections:

> Science is always wrong. It never solves a problem without creating ten more.
>
> —George Bernard Shaw

> Scientists have odious manners, except when you prop up their theory; then you can borrow money from them.
>
> —Mark Twain

Carefully controlled observation lies at the heart of the process, especially concerning the papers reviewed in this book.

> No amount of uncontrolled observation can be a substitute for scientific study.
>
> —Dawber

The problem with uncontrolled observation was amply demonstrated by a professor to a class of young medical students. On the table before him stood a container filled with human urine. The professor's talk dealt with both the importance of utilizing all the body's senses in medical practice and the use of careful observation in clinical practice. "You can learn a great deal by careful observation," he said, dipping a finger into the container of urine, then touching his tongue. The medical students were even more nonplussed (these are modern students, of course, not used to such demonstrations) when the professor ordered everyone to come up and do as he had just done.

We need not dwell on the faces of the quiet, reluctant students as they filed past, one by one, sampling the container. When all were once again seated, the professor reiterated, "Now, let us consider the value of careful observation...you will have noted of course that I dipped this finger in the urine", (holds up index finger), "and I tasted this (holds up middle finger) finger".

The scientific approach to the physical world also implies 1) that if your hypothesis is wrong, you'll get a negative result when you attempt to confirm it; 2) different researchers should be able to get the same results (remembering that errors are also replicable); 3) advocates and critics of a particular hypothesis should agree on what constitutes a 'verification'; 4) the simplest of two equally satisfying explanations takes precedence and finally, extraordinary proof is required for extraordinary claims.

In the field of nutrition, scientists are, unfortunately, the most common offenders against the spirit of true scientific investigation, and bias often enters what should be an open-minded study. Fortunately, giant advances in the field have occurred despite this fact, often due to the inquiries of less biased searchers. In nutrition, however, Planck's assertion that: "...a new scientific truth does not triumph by convincing its opponents and making them see the light, but rather because its opponents eventually die, and a new generation grows up that is familiar with it" often appears substantially correct.

Many of the studies reviewed in this book, especially those conducted in the last ten or fifteen years, have been conducted according to strict rules designed to ascertain that the variable of interest and the factors which influence it are truly interrelated. Statistical methods have been evolved to assist in this task. An example is the cholesterol-heart disease relationship. Although it is known that higher levels of cholesterol in the blood are associated with increased rates of heart attacks, for instance, it has not been clearly shown that this is the cause of the heart attacks or that lowering this variable alone (while continuing to smoke and so on) will prevent cardiac problems. Many factors appear to be involved so extensive, careful studies are required to decipher the causal relationships, to weed out observer errors and bias. D.D. Rutstein, Harvard Medical School said: "The commonest error in reports of clinical research, results from unconscious selection; seek it carefully in reading reports of a study."

Scientists are aware that the methodology of science has its limitations and that other forms of inquiry may be fully as valuable; the human being in his 'scientist' garb hopes to use his method as a guide to wondering inquiry into the functioning of the universe while avoiding the unfortunate condition mentioned by L. Sprague de Camp, a condition often found today wherein: "many people have developed minds that are not only open, but gaping." And much earlier, the great Descartes wrote of his search: "Like those who walk alone and after nightfall, I resolved to proceed so slowly, and with such meticulous circumspection, that if my advance was but small, I should at least guard myself from falling."

In general, this writer feels that 'science' is a very practical and (popularly) underestimated approach to discerning the "Worldly Mysteries," a wondering search to uncover the truths in our material world.

> Science is a first-rate piece of furniture for a man's upper chamber, if he has common sense on the ground floor.
> —Oliver Wendell Holmes

Recognizing that 'common sense is not so common', we'll close with the sentiments expressed by Peter Cook*, who sums up the spirit of a 'true scientist' with, "I am very interested in the Universe. I am specializing in the Universe and all that surrounds it."

General Nutrition

KAABOOOMMM! An incredible explosion about 15 billion years ago marked the beginning of the science of nutrition and signalled the creation of this production we call the Universe. If there had been a night sky, it certainly would have been lit up by this 'Grand Opening.' Recent talk has it that the first few seconds of the life of the Universe were quite impressive—an unbelievably heated mass of expanding matter consisting of the most basic components; no molecules or atoms but just loads of primal gook. Thankfully, this latter material evolved into the simplest elements such as hydrogen and helium. Stars were born and within their cataclysmic cores the heavier elements were created.

GENERAL NUTRITION

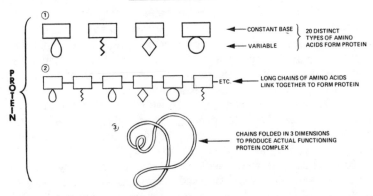

Organic chemistry, father of scientific nutrition, has discovered essential health qualities of food.

---

* Peter Cook is a popular British comedian from such shows as *Beyond The Fringe* and *Pieces of Eight,* as well as appearances on television and Broadway in the U.S.

THE VEGETARIAN'S SELF-DEFENSE MANUAL

This earlier generation of stars eventually died, adding larger amounts of the higher elements to the composition of the Universe. After uncounted years had passed, new stars were formed from this already once digested material and through the same process more and newer elements were formed. The atoms, the actual physical constituents of our bodies, have been through three such stellar digestions. Finally, the earth evolved, and from that thin film on its surface called the ecosphere, we appropriated the atoms and molecules necessary to form our bodies.

The fundamental Second Law of Thermodynamics does not admit to exception, even for living organisms. This Law states that physical and chemical processes tend to increase the 'randomness' of the world. So, in this vast Universe which is tending towards disorder, "living organisms create and maintain (our) essential orderliness at the expense of (our) environment, which (we) cause to become more disordered and random." (Lehninger) Of course, any mother of a 2-year-old child could have told us that.

Lehninger also notes that,

> ...at no point in our examination of the molecular logic of living cells have we encountered any violation of known physical laws, nor have we needed to define new ones. The machinery of living cells functions within the same set of laws that governs the operation of man-made machines, but the chemical reactions and processes of cells have been refined far beyond the present-day capabilities of chemical engineering.

There is no theoretical reason then which should prevent one from fully deciphering the intricacies of both the lives of cells and of the human body as a unit.

Every living organism requires 'food', an intake of materials from the environment to enable growth, replication, maintenance and repair. We, as humans, should consider the air we breathe as 'food', in this sense. Likewise, every living organism requires a source of energy, to bankroll all this activity. Proper functioning of the human body depends upon thousands of compounds, ranging widely in complexity. However, of the above, less than fifty components must be taken in from the environment due to the fact that the body cannot manufacture them itself. Of this small number of essentials, over half consist of 'solitary' elements such as copper, nitrogen, etc. The rest of these essentials consist of the more complex entities such as vitamins and certain amino acids, whose manufacture apparently has the body stumped. The amount of essentials required varies considerably with the age, state, etc., of the body.

Of all the features that the Indian fruit bat and *Homo sapiens* have in common, perhaps the most interesting is that both require a dietary source of vitamin C. Many animals don't require this substance in their diets because they can produce it themselves. In the human, only one additional enzymatic reaction is needed in order to produce vitamin C "in vivo", all the other reactions are already present. In other words, there is very suggestible evidence that for some reason the human body lost the ability to make sufficient amounts of this substance, thus changing it into a dietary essential. It is most reasonable to hope that some day, when scientists are able to locate precisely the area of genetic material or the chromosome which was 'turned off' and thus lost for us this ability, we will be able by some means to 'switch on' once again, thus simplifying the whole nutritional business by requiring one less vitamin.

Many other questions are now raised. If the human body can make many different kinds of amino acids used in its proteins, why should there be eight which, we as adults, must obtain preformed from our food? Have the body's enzyme systems at one time in the past had the ability to make 8 'essential' amino acids and for some reason 'switched off' the appropriate ma chinery? If so, let's switch on again and do away with protein malnutrition in the world. Why can't the human intermediary metabolic systems function like those of certain bacteria who need only very simple substances from the environment and from these are able to build up all other required substances? I is inevitable that one day these systems, if present, will b artificially reactivated. If not present, then perhaps variou biochemical maneuvers will nonetheless still achieve the sam result. The world food problem would not exist if Man coul nourish herself (we must maintain balance) on simpler fare ob tained from the environment. (Algae cookies and a cup of sun shine?) Of course, the best case would still be the availability o chlorophyll implants. Once yearly treatment would enable us t do away with most of what passes for eating, while we simply sit in the sun nourishing ourselves. This would, however, also do away with sunbathing (too fattening!).

Leaving idle speculation far behind, let's briefly examine the actual nutritional requirements of a human vegetarian. The first dietary 'paper' written since the 'Big Bang' billions of years ago, was actually a dietary 'clay'. A clay tablet inscribed 4000 years ago in ancient Sumeria was unearthed, and upon its face was written an appeal from a schoolboy to his mother requesting some bread rolls for supper. He sounds as though he might have been a vegetarian.

From ancient Sumeria, leaping forward several thousand years, we note the development (in the 18th century) of the science of organic chemistry which eventually resulted in the laying of the foundations of scientific nutrition. It was found that food contained certain materials essential to health; carbohydrates, fats, proteins, minerals, and then around the turn of the 20th century 'vitamins' were added to the list. These last few decades of the 20th century, it appears that most substances of major importance in the nutrition of the human body have been discovered. That is not to say, however, that their functions and inter-relationships are at all well-understood or even that the nutritional needs of vegetarians might differ from those of meat-eaters.

Energy

Food has two main functions, the first one being to furnish us with materials for the body's growth, maintenance, and repair. The other major function is to provide us with the energy required to run all our equipment and accessories.

In a fundamental sense, our bodies are fueled by sunshine and constructed of air. Energy, released by tremendously powerful reactions within the sun, constantly bathes the earth, as a broad spectrum of radiation. Plants extract the energy from a narrow portion of this band of radiation by transferring the energy of the sun's photons to electrons (in their chloroplasts). This captured energy is used to construct high energy bonds in certain compounds, such as carbohydrates, that the plant manufactures. Perhaps 90% of the actual mass of a plant (a large tree for instance) is composed of material

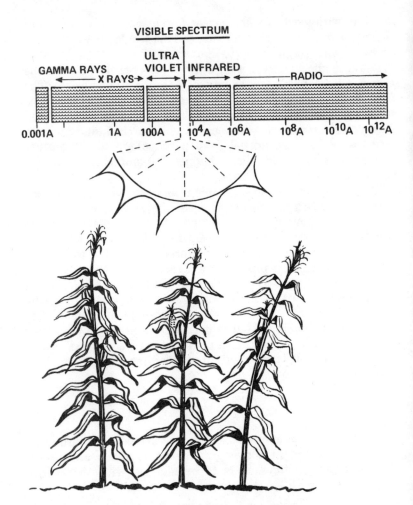

Plants extract energy from sunlight.

taken from the atmosphere. The energy stored in various plant products is in turn a reservoir of potential energy available to any vegetarian who might happen along. The plant food is taken into the body, the high energy bonds are broken and the energy subsequently released is craftily used to run the body's systems while the rest of the substance is used as raw material in various reactions. Thus, in a very direct way, the vegetarian lives on air and sunlight. Eating an animal that has eaten a plant is, at the least, a waste of sunshine and air.

The amount of food energy required by a human being varies considerably, especially with physical activity; however, pregnant state, age, sex, type of diet, body size, etc., all are factors in the final determination. Energy requirements of vegetarians appear to be roughly similar to comparable non-vegetarians (if such exist). Food energy is measured in 'calories'. Intake of too many calories leads to obesity. Therefore, the 'size of the snacks equals the size of the slacks.' Intake of too few calories leads to 'sub-optimal' growth in children, a form of starvation.

The 'problems' which have been raised at one time or another about the nutritiousness of the vegetarian diet deal mainly with a possible nutritional inadequacy of plant protein and a possible lack of certain essential vitamins, mainly vitamin B_{12}', in the vegan diet. This latter substance is discussed in a following chapter; protein we'll discuss briefly below. Carbohydrates (glucose, etc.), have not recently been raised as a problem in the vegetarian diet. Most of the energy stored by plants is packaged as carbohydrates, 'the fuel of life', and a vegetarian diet has an ample supply of these substances. The only 'essential' carbohydrate, a relative of sorts, is ascorbic acid or vitamin C, which was touched on earlier.

Fats

Fats are composed of hydrogen, oxygen, and carbon and have many important functions. Some fats have musical talents (Fats Domino), while others play pool (Minnesota Fats). Dietary fats can serve an energy storage function, aid in the absorption of fat-soluble vitamins (vitamins A, D, E, and K) and serve as material for building various important substances used by the body.

A fat molecule resembles nothing so much as a chandelier with a base composed of a derivative of glycerol and three dangling arms, each arm derived from a 'fatty acid'. Fatty acids consist of chains of carbon atoms strung together like pearls on a string, usually an even number of 'pearls', from 14 to 22 carbon atoms in total. Each of these carbon atoms can form 4 bonds with other atoms; 2 of these bonds, of course, are used simply to connect one carbon atom with the next one above and below it in the chain. Two potential bonds are left. If both the 'extra' bonds of all the carbon atoms in a fatty acid chain are connected to hydrogen atoms then we say the fatty acid is *saturated*. If, on the other hand, only one hydrogen atom is attached to the carbon atom and the fourth available bond is attached to an adjacent carbon atom (either above it or below it in the chain), thus forming a 'double bond', then this fatty acid is said to be 'unsaturated'. The relevance of this is as follows: plant fats contain many unsaturated fatty acids while animal fats contain mainly saturated fatty acids. Consumption of large amounts of saturated fatty acids has been associated with various sorts of epidemic cardiovascular diseases. Protection from these diseases might be related to both decreasing total fat intake and switching to fats containing a greater percentage of unsaturated fatty acids. This is currently a debated topic in several fields.

SECTION ON FATS

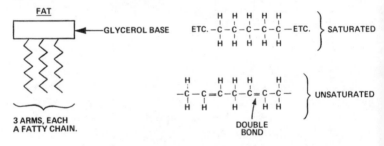

(4) FATTY ACID: CARBON CHAINS, USUALLY 14-22 LONG

Plant fat has unsaturated fatty acids; animal fat has saturated fatty acids

When a fat is taken into the body, the base portion is removed and the fatty acid 'arms' are absorbed separately. While the body can make most fatty acids from other materials just as it can make protein from carbohydrates and vice versa there appears to be one fatty acid which must be taken in the diet of the adult in order to prevent deficiency symptoms, as the body is unable to construct this molecule, at least in the amounts required for normal functioning. The fatty acid is

26

called 'linoleic acid', a chain of 18 carbon atoms containing two double bonds (thus qualifying as a polyunsaturated fatty acid). Some natural vegetable oils contain linoleic acid. It should be noted that human deficiencies of the essential fatty acid have been noted only in those patients who have, for long periods of time, been fed intravenously with mixtures apparently deficient in this compound. Western people in particular, almost certainly take too much fat in their diets and changes from the average of 45% fat in the diet (at present) to perhaps 20% or even less will someday soon be the recommended level of intake.

Protein

Proteins are ubiquitous compounds varying greatly in complexity and performing numerous essential functions in cellular metabolism. Proteins are composed of chains of amino acids, that (to belabor a worn analogy) are strung-together-like-pearls-on-a-string. The string is then folded about in various ways to form compounds of an even greater degree of complexity. Amino acids differ from carbohydrates and fats in that they contain nitrogen. Green plants are able to combine 'inorganic' nitrogen with carbon atoms to produce amino acids. Man, on the other hand, appears unable to manufacture eight types of amino acid in sufficient quantities, and although the body is able to make all the others, it must obtain these eight types via the diet.

There are twenty different amino acids commonly found in proteins. These twenty amino acids may be considered to have two portions, one end is the same in all of them and other end varies from acid to acid, giving each its distinctive character. Amazingly, of the approximately 150 amino acids found in nature, it is always the same 20 that are used as protein building blocks for all forms of life on earth. All twenty amino acids were discovered between 1820 and 1935.

The amounts of the essential amino acids required by the body at various stages of life are under study. The currently recommended amounts of each amino acid are based on the needs of a meat-eating population and, even for them, the figures quoted are considered rather unreliable.

Large protein molecules are not absorbed by the gut to any significant extent but are usually broken down by digestive juices into amino acids which are then selectively absorbed. Any surplus amino acids are burned for energy or transformed into carbohydrates and fats.

Previously, scientists stressed obtaining 'quality' protein in the diet. The 'quality' of a protein depended usually on how well albino rats could grow on the substance. This concept has fallen into disfavor at present. The spotlight now is on the essential amino acid pattern of a protein and on the idea of complementary proteins, the possible amino acid deficiencies of one food supplemented by the surpluses of another type of food. Many completely plant-based protein mixtures have been developed for use in underdeveloped areas where obtaining expensive protein is a problem. These mixtures support the normal requirements of humans at all stages of life.

To make the situation even more interesting, other factors can alter the 'theoretical' essential amino acid pattern of various foods. For example, the way certain cereals are cooked can significantly alter the amounts of the various amino acids released by subsequent digestion in the human gastrointestinal tract. Also, if the body has a surplus of one kind of amino acid such as tyrosine, it can, to a certain extent, use this substance to decrease the requirements for an essential amino acid, phenylalanine. Other examples of this process exist.

Many readers will already have considered the idea that if certain plant foods are low in one or the other of the essential amino acids, then why not simply breed a variety of plant that has a better theoretical amino acid pattern? These genetic manipulations are in progress. A variety of wheat high in lysine has been developed (most wheats are low in that particular amino acid).

The deficiencies of amino acids in certain plant proteins just mentioned, should be considered to be relative. Recommended intakes of amino acids cannot accurately be applied to the individual—vegetarian or not—as far as determining a minimal acceptable intake. Much further research needs to be done. During protein digestion in the gut, the body releases many protein substances which aid digestion but which, because they are themselves protein containing all the essential amino acids, add their own amino acids to the ingested protein and thus sort of stabilize the gut content of amino acids from meal to meal. It is speculated that vegetarians may alter the secretion and reabsorption of these substances so that their requirements for essential amino acids might be considerably different from the 'norm'. Even the idea that a 'complete' protein had to be taken at each meal, because the body couldn't store essential amino acids while awaiting a little more of one or the other to be complete, is now being revised.

One more concept will be encountered ahead, which should be explained to the lay reader. Nitrogen is an essential element found in protein. Nitrogen balance studies are mentioned occasionally later. These studies concern the long-term relationship between nitrogen (protein) intake and nitrogen

"The members of the Vegetarian Society attend their banquet each year in a more and more satisfactory state of health." (Based on an early lithograph by Cham in *Le Charivari*, 16 November 1853)

(protein) loss from the body. A negative nitrogen balance will occur when the dietary protein intake is inadequate or when the diet does not meet the body's energy requirements. Children who are growing rapidly will retain protein in their growing bodies and thus be in positive nitrogen balance if their dietary supplies are adequate. Even though deficiencies of specific essential amino acids, perhaps somewhat surprisingly, do not seem to be associated with any particular evidence of disease, protein-calorie deficiency in general, is the major food problem in the contemporary world.

Millions of healthy vegetarians attest to the virtues of plant protein in sustaining and nourishing their mortal coils. Good sources of plant protein are listed in many books dealing with the diet. Meat..., well, as Reuben states: "It's an excellent source of surprises—most of them unpleasant." He continues on to say that the only thing special about meat is its "tendency to spoil almost instantly with refrigeration. Every essential element can be found better and cheaper in other foods."

All this fuss about protein and amino acids may have given rise to the idea that vast quantities of this substance are required daily. Vegetarians have remained in a completely normal, active condition, taking as little as 10 grams of protein daily. This is less than one-third of an ounce. While most studies on vegetarianism show their intakes to be up around the 70-80 gram level (daily), they may be, as most non-vegetarians are with fat, over consuming an essential dietary element.

Vitamins

Vitamins are complex substances that function as components of important enzyme systems in the body's metabolism. They are required in very small amounts when compared with the required quantities of other essential nutrients, such as amino acids.

The vegetarian in particular should note that special problems can arise when using tables such as the 'Recommended Daily Allowances' in order to determine if one has an adequate diet. Because of the way the tables are constructed, because of individual variations (for example, studies have revealed a three-fold difference in essential amino acid requirements between outwardly similar people) and because of the still insufficiently studied but amazing adaptability of the human organism, the commonly heard comment that "he only met 50 % of the RDA for (whatever) and thus his diet was 'inadequate' are unscientific.

> The human organism has a remarkable versatility in adapting to different food mixtures.... It is important to recognise that dietary adequacy can be obtained with widely different food mixtures. By *adequacy* is meant the level of nutrition that permits achievement of the genetic potential of the individual.
> —Harrison, *Principles of Internal Medicine*

Vegetarianism, once it has achieved a solid scientific foundation, will become the 'norm' in Western nations. A wide variety of plant foods are becoming available, from cauliflower ("a cabbage with a college education") to zucchini. The least one might say is that these foods are less contaminated than flesh foods. A recent headline in U.S. newspapers declared that a variety of carcinogenic compounds, at least 40 in all, were found in ordinary beef. Is this what is meant by having a varied diet?

The scientific investigation of human diet and nutrition continues to turn up new findings. Inter-relationships between various nutrients and the body's handling of them are complex. The whole story of nutrition is, as yet, far from being completely understood. When humanity finally slips away from the confines of our veiled earth, sailing off on its first interstellar voyages, there is little doubt that when the travelers reach some distant new solar system and are brought out of their state of suspended animation, their first meals will be 'three star' vegetarian gourmet. This, of course, will be true only if man has by then not discovered a method of completely circumventing the necessity for eating.

2

THE LITERATURE REVIEWED

The Literature Prior to 1930

This chapter presents, in a more or less chronological fashion, the findings and data unearthed in the scientific investigation of vegetarianism for the years up to 1930. The chronological organization lends itself somewhat to developing a feeling for the progress of scientific concepts as the child—'nutrition'— grew into a science and was applied to the investigation of the vegetarian way of life. If errors of omission have occurred they undoubtedly are in this section dealing with the early years, as the indexing for this time period is frequently incomplete. Many of the earliest references are lifted from Hardinge's papers (who shouldn't mind as he has a whole chapter to himself, later in the book).

Whatever the future of 'science', the past was revolutionary. Great changes in human thought, in our conception of ourselves and our place in the scheme of things, were wrought by the scientific exploration (aided by serendipity) of the world around us. The changes which occurred in medicine were no less dramatic, metamorphosizing the 'leeches' of the past into modern physicians. Many may still say that we are 'leeches' but, personally, I disagree; for all that is good and true in humanity I've seen in full flower in the medical professionals that I've met.

We appreciate that, theoretically, the scientific approach represents an eminently satisfying way of viewing the physical world. Practically, however, it has as its lowest common denominator, the human emotional involvements with the issues, and in matters of diet, vegetarian diet especially, the literature is burdened with unrequited bias, from the earliest days, wherein we might consider it cute and forgivable, to the present when this quality is decidedly less charming and acceptable.

Around 1650 Gassendi studied the teeth of animals and of man. He decided that due to the various similarities, man was related to the herbivorous creatures of the world rather than the carnivorous ones. He was not the first to make this suggestion, however. Not so long thereafter, in 1739, Theophile Lobb, a physician, published his vegetarian blockbuster:

> A Treatise on Dissolvents of the Stone; and on Curing the Stone and Gout by Aliment...Shewing by Reason supported with Experiments, and Cases, the Probability of Dissolving the Stone either in the Kidneys, or Bladder; and of Preventing the Returns of the Gout by suitable Aliment, with proper Rules of Diet.... To which are added Directions of Diet proper for Persons afflicted with Colds, Fevers, Quinseys, Coughs, Asthmas, Cholicks and Pains of the Stomach, Costiveness, Nervous Diseases, Cachexies, Dropsies, Tumours, or Scurvey. The Whole form'd for Usefulness in Families.

Theophile recommended a fleshless dietary as the (non-dissolving) cornerstone of the above most detailed and wonderful cure. A few years later, Cocchi recommended a vegetarian type dietary for disease prevention and good health. Lambe, in 1809, recommended again the same diet for relief from serious disease such as 'Scirrhous Tumours and Cancerous Ulcers'.

William Stark died directly as a result of his nutritional experiments at the age of 29, in 1770. A true scientific spirit is manifest in this Doctor's comments:

> If possibly it could be pointed out to mankind that some articles used as food were hurtful, whilst others were in their nature innocent, and that the latter were numerous, various, and pleasant, they might, perhaps, from a regard to their health, be induced to forego those which were hurtful, and confine themselves to those

which were innocent. To establish such a distinction as this, from experiment and observation, is the chief object of my inquiry: and I confess it will afford me a singular pleasure if I can prove, by experiment, that a pleasant and varied diet is equally conducive to health, with a more strict and simple one; at the same time I shall endeavour to keep my mind unbiased in my search after truth, and if a simple diet seems the most healthy, I shall not hesitate to declare it.

Dr. Stark died of scurvy.

From Dr. M. Hardinge, about whom you will be reading quite a lot, we read:

A prize offered by the Boylston Medical Committee of Harvard University in 1833 for the best thesis on a diet to 'ensure the greatest health and strength to the laborer in the climate of New England', prompted Dr. William A. Alcott of Boston to collect data on the vegetarian regimen.

Hardinge continues:

He was joined in this endeavor by Dr. Milo L. North of Hartford, Connecticut, who published a questionnaire requesting information from those who had adopted such a dietary. The results, including the reports of a large number of medical and other scientific men were published in 1838. The prize, however, had already been awarded to L.V. Bell, who recommended a dietary that included flesh foods.

Dr. Reuben D. Mussey, the fourth President of the American Medical Association, was a strict vegetarian. Schenck remembers meeting him on a trip to Dartmouth College. Dr. Mussey introduced his son, turning his boy about, he said: "feel of him; he has never tasted meat."

Numerous entertaining accounts of the vegetarian lifestyle were written during these years, but strictly speaking they furnish no 'scientific' information of value. See, for example, Mayfield's account of the travails of the vegetarian pioneers in Kansas, 1856.

In 1902, the prestigious *New International Encyclopedia* felt disinclined to favor vegetarianism with a good review.

> Scientific opinion is not favorable to vegetarian-
> ism.... That a mixed diet (i.e., one including
> meat) enables the individual to do more physical
> work and increases the staying powers has often
> been proved. While there are some races that live
> almost exclusively on a vegetable diet, and others
> that exist wholly on animals (for example, the
> Eskimos) it cannot for a moment be contended
> that these are the equals of peoples living on a
> mixed diet.

Encyclopedias have dealt vegetarianism a generally poor hand. Let's look ahead a few years. In the corner on the right, wearing dark brown covers and exemplifying all that is objectionable and unscientific in papers on vegetarians, is an article in the 1970 edition of *Encyclopedia Americana*.

> ...the objections to a strictly vegetable diet are
> based upon the large amount of material required
> to furnish necessary protein, the amount of resi-
> due to be got rid of by the body and the monotony
> of the diet. Most of the so-called vegetarians are
> merely non-meat-eaters.... The fact is that man is
> an omnivorous animal, his digestive apparatus is
> adapted for the digestion of both animal and
> vegetable foods and usually he needs both in
> moderation.

The subsequent portion deals with vegetarianism itself and is composed of quotes, 'assertions' and 'allegations', many of which are actually not that aggravating (everything is relative, of course). Interestingly, of the approximately 25 references used to prepare the article in the 1970 edition only one was published after 1891, and this latter appeared in 1927 in a book by Drews entitled "Unfired Food and Tropho-theraphy." The food may have been unfired but the editor of the *Encyclopedia* should not have been so lucky.

In the corner on the left, wearing red covers and behaving Somewhat less objectionably, is the 1972 edition of *Encyclopedia Britannica*. At least the paper's references are current (well, almost, up to 1959), and the author says nice things like, "Our diet is not imposed by nature: we must choose what to eat", and other provocative statements such as—that many children do not immediately acquire a taste for meat but that it must be developed by repeated exposure to dead muscles and organs he used slightly different words, admittedly).

These intimations of the death of vegetarianism were greatly exaggerated however. Back in 1905, Rymer comments in the *British Medical Journal*:

> Vegetarianism! What is it? In my endeavor to try to enlighten myself and others I have been much struck by the paucity of literature bearing upon it, and what works there are must be termed antiquated, somewhat unscientific, and written with strong bias. The latter characteristic alone renders them unreliable.

Rymer then reviews several findings of the famous Yale professor, Russell H. Chittenden, which were published in his book, *Physiological Economy in Nutrition*. This smash success of 1905 upset many of the entrenched but unvalidated ideas in the young science of nutrition (one being that the average man required over one hundred grams of dietary protein daily—though Chittenden revised this figure drastically downwards). He also performed experiments with athletes, training several omnivorous competitors to live on a vegetarian diet. These athletes went on to compete in the "World's Fair" of 1904 with "complete success."

Rymer impresses one as a careful observer and this characteristic is evidenced in his description of a vegetarian community he studied. He divided the vegetarians into two groups, the first consisting of "Strict Vegetarians" who wouldn't eat meat or fish, and the second composed of those who would allow fish only. He remarked that his experience with the first variety of vegetarian is rather limited and the persons in this group which he observed were what he termed 'faddists' and were unsuited for the diet.

> One case in particular I was able to keep under observation for some years. It was that of a gentleman reduced to the verge of starvation, thin and anemic. His teeth, although not worn were all loose and useless. I strongly advised him to give up this diet, or else his mind and body would give out. He promised to do so, but instead he gave me up.

Rymer had better experiences with the second group of 'vegetarians':

> For some years I have been dental surgeon to a large community of men, numbering some two

hundred.... The Order has been established and carried on without a break for 993 years.... Disease and illness are the exception and from statistics which have been furnished me, I find that the average age they attain is 78 years.

Interestingly, and significantly from a scientific point of view, Rymer notes other important factors which might have affected his findings, such as the regular life led by these people and the fact that a medical exam. was required prior to admission to the Order. His paper concludes that vegetarianism is not harmful to the teeth and that,

> ...we are all aware that in many countries, such as Japan, China, etc., practically no meat has ever been consumed, rice being the chief article of food; by recent events we know that neither mind nor body suffers. A medical gentleman who has lately returned from Japan, after many years of practice in that country, assures me that the general health, including the teeth, is extremely good.

The first in a long series of nefarious articles which have spanned the decades down to the present was published in 1905 (the remarkable year in which Einstein published his special theory of relativity). Some unfortunate soul, desperately ill in one fashion or another because of a starvation diet (which, however, didn't include animal protein), is thus made the subject of a paper entitled "Vegetarianism and ————" (insert here your choice of pitiful conditions). This problem continues in present-day literature. Time seems to have a tendency to amplify this obstacle to a clear appreciation of the sublime beauty of the vegetarian diet.

In this particular paper by Swan, the protagonist was a 20-year-old, third generation vegetarian student with an upper respiratory tract infection, whose diet consisted mainly of rolls and bread made with white flour, occasionally supplemented by a variety of more appealing items. "Metabolism of a Vegetarian" determined that the subject was not receiving enough protein (or calories) and that his diet was:

> ...not calculated to produce a properly nourished and mentally and bodily active individual.... The average book, pamphlet, or magazine article advocating vegetarianism, so far as I have been able

> to examine such, contains no accurate scientific
> analysis of the requirements of the human organ-
> ism, and the arguments advanced for the
> adoption of such a regimen are pseudo-scientific
> or sentimental.

One must agree with Swan's last statement.

The 1910 edition of the *Encyclopedia Britannica* discussed vegetarianism in a relatively balanced fashion. The article postulates five main reasons for becoming a vegetarian and I'd like to note the last one:

> Character Improvement—on the ground that
> after the virtues of courage and valour and fear-
> lessness have been taught in the lower stages of
> evolution, the virtue of gentle humaneness and
> extended sympathy for all that can suffer should
> be taught in the higher cycles of the evolutionary
> spiral. Flesh-eating entailing necessarily an im-
> mense volume of pain upon the sentient creation
> should be abstained from by the 'higher classes'
> in the evolutionary scale.

This article also mentions many prominent vegetarians of the day, athletes, competing at the championship levels in many sports, a disproportionate number of them being successful in the endurance events such as 100-mile cycle races.

Annoyingly, even at this time, vegetarians were often termed 'cultists' or 'faddists' by those working in nutritional science, such as it was. An unknown author writing in the *British Medical Journal* (1911) states:

> Nor have the therapeutic and dietetic uses of
> vegetables been left to be discovered by modern
> faddists. At the present day the banana and the
> potato are held in high repute by some physicians
> as adjuvants in the treatment of rheumatism; the
> potato has, moreover, been raised by a French
> physician to the rank of a specific for diabetes....
> The potato helps to maintain the mental equilib-
> rium. It may therefore be prescribed to enthusi-
> asts of all kinds. The remedy, however, must not
> be abused, as too much potato—and this we can

> well believe—causes in the patient the develop-
> ment of a desire to do nothing. This action
> might, however, have a distinct advantage in the
> case of too ardent reformers—The system would
> seem to have been partly foreshadowed by
> Gilbert in *Patience*, where Bunthorne sings that:
> "A sentimental passion of a vegetable fashion
> must excite your languid spleen."

One year after the first, incredible, Great War began, we encounter the first scientific study of the metabolism of non-starved vegetarians. Two researchers, Benedict and Roth, point out that "in the discussion of the supposed benefits of vegetarianism, considerable stress has been laid upon the re-markable endurance apparently shown by vegetarians over flesh-eaters, the statement being made that the vegetarians live upon a distinctly lower metabolic plane, are not so highly stim-ulated as the flesh-eaters, have a lower blood pressure, and, in general, that the metabolic activities are on a lower level—It is perfectly feasible to measure the metabolic plane by studying the respiratory exchange." One might consider metabolism as everything that is the end result of nutrition, the building up and the tearing down of bodily tissues and the net resultant state of the body. Now, this is a home grown explanation (so please don't write if you disagree) but it's close to the truth. A handful of vegetarians were borrowed from Dr. J.K. Kellogg of cornflake and Battle Creek fame. After conducting a fairly care-fully controlled experiment with the 22 subjects, the research-ers concluded "that living on a vegetarian diet for a longer or shorter period does not fundamentally alter the basal gaseous metabolism." So nothing here for the vegetarian to brag about, unless you enjoy being 'normal'. Later studies, reviewed in other chapters, reveal other results regarding metabolism.

The reader was earlier promised that this book would deal almost solely with the scientific literature on human vegetar-ians although we will now make a short but necessary detour to deal with a small, white creature—the albino rat—who, through his general inability to live on the vegetables provided him or her in experiments, produced the impression in many workers' extrapolating minds, that the vegetarian diet was also unfit for humans.

"Why won't you eat your peas? They're good for you."

Rats!

McCollum, who was later to discover Vitamin A and who also made many other contributions to nutritional science, stated in 1916 that:

> ...the prevalence of pellagra in the United States during recent years, and the accumulation of evidence that it is induced by a faulty diet, chiefly of plant origin, has aroused an interest never before equalled in the question of the adequacy of the strictly vegetarian diet. In the present paper we desire to discuss the vegetarian diet in the light of an extensive experience in feeding restricted diets to several species of animals. Testimony as to the favorable results of human experience with what are purported to be strictly or practically vegetarian diets are so untrustworthy as to merit little confidence,...

He mentions some experiments performed by Slonaker, who was attempting to raise some rather sickly vegetarian rats.

McCollum was almost unique in his success in raising vegetar
ian rats.

> Our practically complete success in the nutrition
> of rats with strictly vegetarian diets made up of
> but three natural foodstuffs and the failure at-
> tending the employment of a wider variety in the
> food mixture, emphasizes the fallacy of the as-
> sumption that the safest plan to ensure perfect
> nutrition, is to include a wide variety in the
> selection of the constituents of the diet.... As
> soon as we possess an adequate knowledge of the
> specific properties of our natural foodstuffs and
> their supplementary relations to each other, it
> will certainly be possible to compound fairly
> simple and monotonous diets which can be
> depended upon to induce physiological well-being
> closely approximating the optimum. The consci-
> entious adherence to a vegetarian diet by one who
> has no adequate technical knowledge regarding
> the subject of diet appears to be fraught with
> danger since among the foods of vegetable origin,
> ordinarily consumed by human beings, several
> dietary factors are as a rule of an unsatisfactory
> chemical character. It is certain that all the
> components of a successful diet are present in
> foods of plant origin.

Subsequently, great volumes of studies by Kanai, Kestner,
Kaunitz, Chang, Chen, Luo, Lin, Tang, Wan, Wu, and others,
in various combinations, revealed that vegetarian rats, when
compared with omnivorous ones:

> —cost less to feed
> —weighed less
> —grew poorly
> —died early on raw pea diets
> —developed cataracts
> —the males learned poorly (who'd run a
>   maze for a raw pea??)
> —died younger generally
> —lived longer generally

and many other, often contradictory findings. While we can
sympathetically conclude, as Carlson did in 1947, that "a
purely vegetarian diet satisfactory for albino rats therefore still
remains to be found," the reader should realize that much

'misinformation' results from these studies and that prestigious medical journals often uncritically jumped to false conclusions on the basis of them. Let me quote evidence from two such editorials, both in the *Journal of the American Medical Association*. The first published in 1928, began in fine open-minded fashion:

> The modern critics of the vegetarian propaganda have frequently overlooked the fact that this doctrine has repeatedly, if not always, been the expression of an ethical movement among its expounders, and that its development and transformation ought to be considered with reference to sociological, economic and ethical conditions as well as from the standpoint of physiology.... While some of the arguments offered in sober earnestness in support of abstinence from flesh foods are suggestive of mental invalidism, others demand serious consideration and an answer based on scientific understanding. It would be utterly unwarranted to maintain that vegetarianism is a physiologic impossibility. Thousands of devotees stand ready to refute such an assertion by the example of their own experiences. The real problem, from a nutritional standpoint, centers in the alleged superiorities of the vegetarian regimen.

Very interesting: but then, after reviewing the rat studies, the paper concludes:

> Since the metabolism of the rat has been shown to be similar to that of the human being, who also for many thousands of years has been omnivorous, it seems justifiable to the Chinese experimentors to conclude that optimal nutrition of human beings cannot be obtained with purely vegetarian diets.

The second paper (1935) concludes basically that the strict vegetarian diet is deficient, based in large degree on the rat studies. Now, if elephants would fit into laboratory cages a little more handily, we should probably have lots of evidence that vegetarian fare does indeed support life. Many of the early "scientific" arguments against vegetarianism were based on the nutritional studies with these little white rats as subjects. Even modern concepts such as "complete protein" (falling into disfavor at present), recommended daily allowances of various food elements, etc., owe much to extrapolations from studies of these creatures. The room for error and false deductions is great. Meanwhile, returning to the first Great War...

*

- -

*

No new scientific data are presented in Keith's paper (1916), 'Is Vegetarianism Based on Sound Science', but is nonetheless a fair exposition of the problem as it was viewed in those days. In her introduction she states:

> Although vegetarianism has been taken up frequently from reasons which may be called emotional, there is also much testimony as to great improvement in the physical condition of those who have adopted it. For instance, of Sarah Bernhardt it is said that she has 'demonstrated' that a vegetarian diet makes one younger and more elastic and gives a clear brain and steady nerve.... August Rodin, the sculptor, considers that his imagination works more clearly and the general tone of his production is higher.

I ask the reader, could it be that it is not the Cosmic Mystery but rather a vegetable casserole which is the object of 'The Thinker's contemplation'? (In the interest of fairness regarding the mental clarity derived from a vegetarian diet, it should be noted that Swift attributed a "strange vertigo in my head" to the eating of too much fruit. Perhaps *Gulliver's Travels* is the result of an overdose of bananas).

The Great War ground on and, like most wars, was a great unnatural experiment in the nutrition of millions of people due to deficiencies secondary to the upheavals in normal life that the hostilities caused. Beginning several years before the turn of the century, extending through the war and continuing for several years thereafter, a number of interesting papers were published by a vegetarian, the Danish scientist Hindhede, the 'bicycling professor'. A member of the Danish Wartime Food Commission, he was quoted in 1915 as saying that the most dangerous of the forces with which Germany had to contend was the German pig. To feed grain and potatoes to cattle and swine in order to eat meat, meant the loss of at least 80% of the food's nutritional value. With this in mind, in Denmark, the Food Commission instituted a policy of reserving the vast majority of grains for direct human consumption with the resultant adequate provision of food for all in the country during those troubled times. Hindhede asserted: "The German soldiers conquered France in 1871 with the aid—or in spite of—three-fourths of a pound of meat a day, and they went into the present war on the same basis. Germany has paid a high penalty...". In a subsequent paper, he summarizes his findings on the Danish wartime diets:

> The Danish food regulation (low protein, low fat, lots of bran) was a most interesting problem for me. It was a low protein experiment on a large scale, about 3,000,000 subjects being available.... During the year of regulation it (the death rate from all diseases which had remained stable since 1900) showed a decrease of 34%. It would seem, then, that the principal cause of death lies in food and drink.... This result was not a surprising one for me. Since 1895, when I began my experiments with a low protein diet (mostly vegetarian), I have been convinced that better physical conditions resulted from this standard of living. It may be said that a vegetarian diet is a more healthful diet than the ordinary diet.

Quoting McCollum, Hindhede continues:

> Lacto-vegetarianism should not be confused with strict vegetarianism. The former is, when properly planned, the most highly satisfactory plan which can be adopted in the nutrition of man.

Of his own feelings he wrote:

> While not all readers will agree with what I have said, no one can dispute the fact that the people of Denmark have no cause to regret that during the war their diet consisted mostly of milk, vegetables and bran...

While it has *not* been shown, as of the date of this book, that man (or woman) requires flesh foods in order to be properly nourished, what happens if one survives on an exclusively meat diet? This gruesome topic will be considered here if only for its novelty value for the future, all vegetarian, generations. A paper by Lieb details his studies of Vilhjalmur Stefansson, the Arctic explorer. This gent was in fairly good shape, both physically and mentally. He lived for up to nine months at a time on an exclusively flesh food diet with no apparent ill effects.

The second paper, 1889, is by Herschell, who studied some 'savages', cannibals from Terra del Fuego, who were being 'exhibited at the Westminster Aquarium'. This family lived on flesh foods and water only. Herschell must have had to time his visits judiciously, for the savages "...take hardly any exercise at all. They spend most of their time in sleep." Of course, the constant sleeping may have been due, not their dietary habits, but to jet-lag (or the 1880s equivalent—*ship*-lag?).

Other papers from these years (up to 1930) are reviewed in subsequent appropriate chapters. The reader probably has discovered by now that there was not really that much truly scientific information on vegetarianism discovered during these decades. Because of the strong ethical and moral implications of the diet, however, this lack of information did not in the least impede discussion of the "vegetarian problem." In all fields, the years which followed (1930-1950) were ones of incredible developments, the enormously important discovery and development of antibiotics, the discovery of food factors such as Vitamin B_{12} and the discovery of Bing Crosby?

1930 to 1954

A great deal of interest in human physiology and metabolism was sparked by the isolation of the hormone *insulin*, in 1922. This general stimulation had a beneficial fallout upon the studies in which we are interested. Human nutrition turned out to be much more fascinating and complex than even the most visionary of the early nutritionists could have dreamed. Not only did the tools of investigation become progressively more accurate, but the approach to the data sought was honed to a sharp edge; studies required 'devices' to make certain that the conclusions were valid and not unduly influenced by factors which were not accounted for. Statistics also came to the aid of the scientists, certain well-known quotes notwithstanding ("There are three kinds of lies: lies, damned lies, and statistics."), although the major impact of statistical studies began later, in 1960s.

This section is relatively short, due to the review of a number of pertinent papers published during these decades elsewhere, in the appropriate chapters. In order to provide some continuity, we'll return to 1921 for our first paper, "The Meatless Diet" by Frank. This paper is so sensible that it should have actually been written later, to coincide with the spirit of modern times. Frank was the superintendent of the Beth Israel Hospital in New York City who wished to convert his hospital to an all-plant food diet so that the food would automatically be kosher. "Scientifically, one cannot say the meat is a necessary ingredient in the human dietary." Frank did not include fish in his definition of 'meat'. Any meat that would be served in the hospital had to be authorized by a physician's prescription. In order to ensure that this diet would not be harmful, Frank wrote to the leading contemporary scientists working in fields related to physiology and nutrition — Mendel, Chittenden, Lusk, McCollum, Benedict, and Vaughan. The essence of their replies are as follows:

a) Benedict: "Looking out for the food accessory substances (which we now call vitamins, essential amino acids, etc.), I should be quite inclined to feel that your plan was a safe one."

b) Chittenden: "...I beg to state that in my opinion it is quite possible, and indeed a desirable thing, for many reasons, to establish a lacto-vegetarian dietary in the wards of your hospital. There is no question in my mind that such a diet can be made nutritious and healthful." (Yale)

c) McCollum: "I have not the slightest hesitation in saying that vegetarian diet, supplemented with fairly liberal amounts of milk, is the most satisfactory type of diet that man can take." (Johns Hopkins)

d) Mendel: "I have given some thought to the advisability of introducing a meatless dietary. ...there will be no objection on physiological grounds...I myself lived upon a diet devoid of meat, fowl, and fish for nearly a year, for purely experimental purposes, and remained in excellent health and vigor..." (Yale)

The other respondents were of the same mind. The names above represent an all-star collection from the galaxy of American science. Frank concluded his paper by reaffirming his desire to make this important change in the hospital dietary. "We have yet to be convinced that there is any good in a meat dietary for a hospital treating acutely ill patients."

Studies by Klewitz, Eimer, and Holmgren demonstrated (to their satisfaction, at least) that vegetarians met their protein requirements on the diet, that athletes did well on the diet, and that the diet protected one against the desire to overeat, overseason, to drink, and to smoke. Actually the only time vegetarians seem to smoke is when they run too fast. Perhaps that's why many of them enjoy water sports.

Is it only coincidence, the association between an author's name and the subject he or she writes upon? A textbook of neurology by Brain, of dentistry by Paine and now—Muley, who investigated the vegetarian porters at the docks in Istanbul. He found that they tended to suffer less from such diseases as arthritis, thrombosis, and cancer (types unspecified), than their meat-eating compatriots.

The vegetarian [on high protein diet] has endurance.

Turning to the sports scene, we make note of an epic contest between vegetarians (wearing the white hats) and meat-eaters (wearing the black hats). Norgaard checked out a 50-kilometer walking match which pitted 12 flesh-eaters against 12 vegetarians. Both teams did reasonably well but the vegetarians lost more weight, on an average, during the course of the race than did the meat-eaters. "Two of the participants collapsed during the match. Although the collapse was severe (one meat-eater and one vegetarian) there was no change in the urea or glucose content of the blood, but the calcium concentration was increased." Unfortunately, for the edification of our more competitive readers, Norgaard fails to indicate to whom went the victory.

The Vegetarian Athletic Club of Glasgow collaborated with Wishart in 1934, in order to study a 48-year-old cyclist who had been a vegetarian for 23 years. Wishart's main difficulty lay in providing a pure vegetable diet of high protein content "in amounts that were readily digestible", so some of his diets included milk and eggs. His subject, an Olympic-class competitor, was in fine shape; he had biked 402.5 miles in 24 hours in 1921. Wishart was interested in how he utilized protein and found that he did best on a high protein diet but that it was difficult to obtain with the foods available to him. Modern commerce, providing an abundance and variety of vegetarian foods, renders this problem of Wishart's obsolete.

Perhaps only peripherally related to our main subject, the paper by Mauriac (1935) is nonetheless quite interesting. He had six patients who required insulin to control their blood sugars, juvenile diabetics. He switched them back and forth between a "standard" diet and one containing green vegetables, in any desired amounts. Mauriac found that on the latter diet his patients' insulin requirements were reduced to one half of their former levels. While he provided no information to show that both diets resulted in similar caloric intakes (calorie restriction can influence the amount of insulin required for a specified level of control) these findings correlate well with a recent paper in the *Journal of the American Medical Association*, which purported to show that increasing the amount of vegetable fiber in diets of insulin-dependent diabetics consistently lowers their insulin requirements. Anecdotally, a friend of this writer, a juvenile diabetic, noted a sustained decrease of approximately 50% in her insulin requirements, this coincident with the adoption of a balanced vegetarian diet. A long-term study of these impressions, to document their possible reality, would certainly be interesting.

Vegetarians are inveterate proselytizers. If the reader finds herself or himself in this category and if in the course of a diet-related conversation, no progress has been made in convincing those not in the fold of the ethical, moral, and nutritional benefits of the diet—let me introduce you to Kaunitz. His research disclosed this remarkable bit of information: "Patients on a vegetarian diet had much less flatulence than those on a mixed diet and the flatus contained much more CO_2." So, since this latter gas is much less flammable than other gases found in flatus, we may add to the arguments in favor of vegetarianism (should this discovery be substantiated, of course), that vegetarians are much ~~more socially acceptable~~ less of a fire hazard than meat-eaters.

We are sending Adolph (for his opening statement anyway), a free one year's home study course by "prophetess" Jeane Dixon. His paper is interesting but his opening prediction in 1939 has missed the mark:

> Rural China has furnished what is probably the best large-scale, long-term experiment with a vegetarian diet which the modern world has witnessed. Vegetarian fads in our Occident have come and gone and, while enthusiasts still stage occasional revivals, it is probable that as an accepted nutritional regimen, pure vegetarianism is on the wane.... It is of no small moment to realize that this large rural community of several hundred million people has lived and survived for, say, 40 centuries without milk as food and without the use of any kind of dairy industry. Nor can it be asserted that the net result of this national experiment is qualitatively inferior, for example, to that of the Mongols to the north of the Chinese who do consume milk. Nor is this result in any sense culturally inferior to that of non-vegetarian cultures.

We'll close this chapter with one last paper, a work by Groen, which introduces us to the "Vegetarian of the Year." He describes two patients. His first patient was an unfortunate, thirty-three-year-old physical disaster whose atrocious diet was exceeded only by her atrocious health. While some of us, if it weren't for ill-health would have no health at all, this poor soul, gave even ill-health a bad name. Although she enters the literature as a 'vegetarian', she does not deserve to be labeled as such simply because her diet was lacking in meat.

The second patient, the one referred to as the "Vegetarian of the Year", wins the title on the basis of effort alone. She was an engaging fourteen-year-old who came from a family who "lived under extremely poor financial conditions. The family had always been vegetarian. Two years ago after the patient's father had died, it became increasingly difficult for them to maintain a varied vegetable diet on this low income. Finally, the family ate chiefly bread, oleomargarine, and brown sugar, but three or four times a week they had vegetables and potatoes. After one year of this diet they all felt so weak that they gave up the vegetarian regime. Our little girl, however, had always disliked meat and kept to her vegetarian principles." The persevering youngster maintained her deficient (fleshless) diet but when seen at the clinic showed evidence of malabsorption. She was switched to a more nutritious diet which was, unfortunately (from our point of view), a mixed diet, and recovered some of her health. A noble effort nonetheless, proving that it's not the size of the dog in the fight but rather the size of the fight in the dog that really matters.

As our present century passed the halfway mark, nutritional studies regarding vegetarians, in general, attained new levels of excellence (like rising from penury to abject poverty). Very little anecdotal information was published, measurement and experiment having taken over from the less reliable ways of gathering information. Despite this, we are still reminded, that even assembled facts mean little when not viewed in the true spirit of science.

All the remaining studies in this book are categorized by topic of interest rather than chronologically. These last two sections have been really only an introduction to the papers that follow.

1954 and All That

The studies of Hardinge, Stare, and Crooks are the peanut butter in the great vegetarian sandwich of life. An investigation of a group of 200 subjects, two-thirds of whom were vegans and vegetarians, was published as a series of six papers spanning more than a decade, bringing before us a large body of new information on vegetarianism and resulting in Mervyn G. Hardinge, M.D. becoming Mervyn G. Hardinge, M.D., Ph.D. Although in other chapters we will touch on topics raised in this review, it would be helpful to consider these papers as a unit without too much adulteration by other wonder-filled facts related to vegetarianism. Listed below are Hardinge's articles.

1. Nutritional Studies of Vegetarians: nutritional, physical, and laboratory studies (1954)
2. Nutritional Studies of Vegetarians: dietary and serum levels of cholesterol (1954)
3. Nutritional Studies of Vegetarians: dietary levels of fibre (1958)
4. Nutritional Studies of Vegetarians: dietary fatty acids and serum cholesterol levels (1962)
5. Non-Flesh Dietaries: a) Historical Background (1963)
    b) Scientific literature (1963)
    c) Adequate and inadequate diets (1964)
6. Nutritional Studies of Vegetarians: proteins and essential amino acids. (1966)

One might ask Hardinge, why study a subject so obscure as vegetarians if you are seriously trying to bag a Ph.D? To that he replies:

> Additional knowledge as to the nutritional requirements of human beings may be gained by a study of those who have unique dietary habits. The vegetarian groups in the United States afford an opportunity to observe the effect of such 'natural experiments'. Experimental studies in this field have generally been for short periods of time, and of the few surveys made, many were conducted in areas of the world where poor economic conditions greatly curtail the amount and type of foods eaten. It was, therefore, believed that a comparative study of vegetarians, made in times and areas of relative plenty, among people who have voluntarily selected their dietary regimes, and who have pursued these practices

for years, lifetimes, and even generations, would contribute valuable information to the present knowledge of nutrition.

Stare and Crooks along with Hardinge, briefly reviewed the past literature (however, with none of the ranting and raving found in this book). They mention Yukawa, who found the vegetarian monks in Japan to be in good health; and Taylor, whose studies of Eastern soldiers during World War II merits the comment that "Limitation in the availability of fruits, vegetables, and milk which was to replace the meat in the vegetarian diet handicapped the vegetarians especially." Finally, they mention Jaffas's study, published in 1901, dealing with a fruitarian family who were in good health but smaller than average, possibly due to heredity.

Who were Hardinge's subjects? He states:

> The subjects selected for this study were adolescents, preganant women, and men and women 45-70 years of age.... Three classes of subjects were sought for each group, namely lacto-ovo-vegetarians, 'pure' vegetarians, and non-vegetarians.... The vegetarian groups, as far as possible, were selected first, and then from the much larger population of non-vegetarians the respective control groups were formed. Age, because of its tangible nature, was used as the criterion for the latter selection, the ages of the subjects in respective groups being approximately matched.... All subjects were of the white race, of average or above average social and economic levels, and considered themselves to be in good health. All had voluntarily maintained their respective dietaries from a minimum of five years preceding the study to throughout life.

Pertaining to Hardinge's first paper in a nutshell, he found no significant differences between his groups for the items under study:

> The results show that although the dietary intake of nutrients varied widely among individuals, the average intake of all groups, with the exception of the adolescent 'pure' vegetarians, approximated or exceeded the amounts recommended by the National Research Council. Non-vegetarian adolescents consumed significantly more protein than did lacto-ovo-vegetarian and 'pure' vegetar-

ian adolescents...however this larger protein intake was not reflected in greater growth as measured by height. No evidence was obtained to indicate that a lacto-ovo-vegetarian diet failed to provide an adequate dietary for an expectant mother.... In general, measurements of height, weight, and blood pressures of these groups showed no significant differences. However, the 'pure' vegetarians weighed appreciably less, an average of 20 pounds. Preconception and postpartum weight gains and losses of the pregnant women were similar, as were the average birth weights of infants among the lacto-ovo-vegetarians and non-vegetarians. The total protein, albumin and globulin values, and the hematological findings for all the vegetarian and non-vegetarian groups were not statistically different."

For the interest of medical people and the probable bewilderment of all others, the hematological parameters measured and found similar in all groups were the ESR, WBC with differential, HCT, RBC and red cell indices—MCV, MCHC, MCH.

Cholesterol, cholesterol, always cholesterol

A theory originating with the Russians back in the early 1900s, postulated that cholesterol was an agent with a tendency to cause blood vessel disease and heart attacks. People, alarmed, subsequently reduced their intakes, switched diets, and attempted in any way possible to reduce their serum cholesterol levels and thus hopefully reduce their chances for a premature translation to the ethereal realms. Most workers now feel that there is still much to be learned in this regard and for most Western people, preventing heart attacks is somewhat more complex than was originally thought. Cholesterol was widely studied in the 1950s, '60s, and '70s and it is in this context that Hardinge's second paper should be read. Mention of cholesterol also allows us to provide the average reader (no insult intended, I only mean other than medical professionals) with the chemical description of cholesterol below, which is sure to inflame your sensibilities (every book deserves at least one section of unmitigated profundity).

'Sterols' are a class of steroids and steroids are derivatives of the perhydrocyclopentanophenanthrene nucleus. Cholesterol is the most abundant sterol in human tissue and can occur as either the free alcohol or in a combined form. We obtain it from both our diet and our body, the latter manufacturing large amounts of the substance. Plants contain other sterols but do not contain cholesterol. Thus the cholesterol in the bloodstream of a vegan, who takes no animal products, is strictly of local manufacture.

Cognizant of the smaller number of subjects used in gathering data for this paper, we can summarize Hardinge's results as follows:

a) Vegans had significantly lower serum cholesterol levels than were found in vegetarians, who in turn had lower levels than meat-eaters (although in the adolescent-age groups the differences were not significant).

b) Cholesterol levels appeared more closely related to the intake of animal fat than to total fat intake.

c) No relationship between body weight and serum cholesterol was found.

d) Whether significant or not, no cases of high blood pressure were found in vegans, whereas cases were found in the other two groups.

Despite the fact that moral fibre as yet cannot be measured in the lab, scientists have not been deterred from studying dietary fibre. This latter substance (we won't define the term) is presently a hot topic, being touted in one circle or another as the cure for everything from cancer to constipation. Much of the recent interest stems from the colonic evangelism of Dr. Denis Burkitt who equates the high fibre diets of various native cultures with their low rates of bowel cancer. This writer was fortunate enough to attend one of Dr. Burkitt's talks several years ago when he visited Alberta, and I'm able to testify to his remarkable gift for proselytizing, which was exceeded only by his even more remarkable color slides of stool samples he'd gathered from the far corners of the earth. This well-known gentleman noted some of the problems he encountered on his field trips in various countries, the indigenous population perhaps a bit alarmed with his peculiar (even for an Englishman) fascination in collecting said samples.

Hardinge and his group found that lacto-ovo-vegetarians consumed 50% more fibre than non-vegetarians and that vegans consumed yet another 80% more than the vegetarians. All groups were free of gastrointestinal complaints. The authors speculate that: "...it is possible that the increased fibre content of the vegetarian diets reported here may have played some role in the lower cholesterol levels observed, though we have no direct evidence of this."

If you've forgotten what fatty acids are, review the simplistic explanation in the section on nutritional factors. Then you'll be ready for the following conclusions reached by Hardinge in 1962.

1. In the older age groups, the higher the dietary intake of unsaturated fats (these form a high percentage of the fats in the diets of vegans and vegetarians), the lower the serum cholesterol levels.

2. In the same age group, ingestion of large amounts of animal fats were associated with high cholesterol levels and low serum cholesterol levels were associated with a high intake of polyunsaturated fatty acids.

3. In the youngest age groups, despite differences in the dietary intake of fats and fatty acids, there was no significant difference between all the groups (i.e., vegan, vegetarian, meat-eaters) in relation to the serum cholesterol level.

So, in general, it appears that anyone past their teens, who wishes to lower their serum cholesterol level, would do well by adopting the eating habits of the humble vegan. What benefit (other than bliss) this would bring is purely speculative at present.

Much of what Hardinge presents in his next three papers on "Non-Flesh Dietaries" is found in other chapters in this book. We'll consider a few findings noted in the last of this series of three:

> Widely differing dietary practices appear among vegetarians and near-vegetarians. A reasonably chosen plant diet, supplemented with a fair amount of dairy products, with or without eggs, is apparently adequate for every nutritional requirement of all age groups. Pure vegetarian diets, the use of which produced no detectable de-

ficiency signs, contained adequate calories obtained mainly from unrefined grains; legumes; nuts and nut-like seeds; a variety of vegetables, including the leafy kinds; and usually an abundance of fruits.

Vegetarian and near-vegetarian diets that have proved inadequate include a) vegan diets which have been reported to produce Vitamin B_{12} deficiency in some individuals; b) grossly unbalanced near-vegetarian diets in which as much as 95% of the calories were provided by starchy foods extremely low in protein, such as cassava root; c) diets dependent too largely on refined cereals, such as cornmeal or white rice, even though small amounts of animal foods were included; and d) intake of total calories insufficient for maintenance requirements.".

In regard to point a) above, see section on B_{12} for more up-to-date information on the subject. Hardinge notes:

The results are not uniform. Some individuals appear to maintain good health for many years or practically a lifetime, without developing symptoms of deficiency. Others are forced to use supplementary vitamin B_{12} or revert to a lacto-ovo-vegetarian diet after a few months or a few years. The reason for this variation is not clear.

The final paper from the hands of Hardinge et al. to be considered here, was published in 1966 and concerned itself with the protein and essential amino acid intake of their subjects. They found that all the groups involved "met and generously exceeded twice their minimum requirements" for the essential amino acids, with the non-vegetarians having the highest intakes in most cases.

So we have arrived at the end of this review of Hardinge's nutritional investigations, begun in that wonderful year of 1954. However, lest 1954 be remembered as the year that clear thinking intruded into the question of the nutritional status of vegetarians, we should note a paper of Sebrell:

Vegetarian diets should probably be placed in this category—fads derived from fear of foods. Behind the early writings on the subject, one can usually discern the idea that meat arouses animal passions and is therefore inimical to philosophic and spiritual thought. Nutritionists do not challenge the statement that humans can subsist on a non-meat diet, but foods must be selected with great care if a proper balance of nutrients is to be obtained. Among vegetarian races, signs of protein deficiency are frequent, whereas a heavy meat diet is quite compatible with good health and development.

Life is actually somewhat simpler as regards the reasons for becoming vegetarian. Many people feel that if your potential meal can out-run or out-swim you, it's better to switch your dietary selections to more sedentary forms of life. All the evidence we've seen really indicates that it's alright to become a vegan or a vegetarian when a normal varied diet is taken. Speaking defensively, we can state that your health will not suffer for the change. Personally, I've seen a number of cases, who, following a switch to vegetarian fare, broke out in violent attacks of good health, followed by bouts of physical exercise and sweet thoughts. I myself was nearly overcome, and narrowly escaped by following the advice of Mark Twain (again) regarding exercise, that is to simply lie down and be still until the passion for exercise passes over.

3

SMALL AND
FRUITFUL SUBJECTS

Motherhood and Pregnancy

Considering the number of years that vegetarians have been available in childbearing models, the scarcity of scientific papers dealing specifically with vegetarianism and pregnancy is almost inconceivable. While we've just noted that Hardinge found his vegetarian ladies to have absolutely normal pregnancies and children, this was many years ago. By the 1970s, this fertile field of research, which should really have given birth to numerous scientific studies, had produced only three for presentation to the reader. The attitudes which give rise to this deficiency appear impregnable to change and this is rather difficult to bear. Despite this, let's review the information that is available and see what the fruits of our labor will be. It should be noted that snipets of information on pregnancy are scattered throughout many of the other chapters. We are concerned here only with quality papers dealing exclusively with this subject.

The 1951 studies by Sheft and Oldham included thirteen pregnant subjects, seven of whom were lacto-ovo-vegetarian, and for this reason we'll review them here. The authors studied the effect the caloric intake had on how the body used the protein in the diet (nitrogen utilization). On self-selected diets, all the subjects except one, a vegetarian, ate less than the recommended number of calories daily (2400) and in all the ladies the nitrogen utilization was low. These women all had normal deliveries and at 20 months all the children were healthy. The authors of that study comment that the low nitrogen utilization was due to the low caloric intake rather than some problem with the nitrogen intake.

These same two authors studied the amino acid intakes and reported the results the following year. Their conclusion was that the vegetarians were no different than non-vegetarians as far as the intakes of amino acids was concerned. They felt that intake of methionine was marginal in vegetarians (based on RDA).

A fair number of studies exist which might be considered for review here because their subjects were pregnant 'vegetarians', are rejected because the 'vegetarians' dealt with lived on subsistence diets for reasons of poverty and other factors. Thus we are left with only one last paper to review. Dent and Gupta studied pregnancy in Asian immigrants to England who were vegetarian and compared them with non-vegetarian Asians and 'Caucasians'. A severe disease of pregnancy called osteomalacia ('soft bones') is due to Vitamin D deficiency. Their study is important from more than just the vegetarian viewpoint. Let the authors explain.

> The modern view is that calcium deficiency is relatively unimportant in such complications of pregnancy but that Vitamin-D deficiency remains extremely important at least for the baby.... In consequence, measures to supplement the diet of pregnant women with extra vitamin D have been recommended and fitfully adopted. Although not proven, the usual view remains that pregnancy does probably increase the requirement of vitamin D...The Nutrition Board, U.S.A., recommend an intake of 400 IU (10 ug) daily during pregnancy and lactation. An average English diet provides about 100 IU of vitamin D so is just sufficient to maintain health under ordinary circumstances. The intake of the Asian vegetarian is, however, much lower and they are less prone to augment this by exposing their skin to the sun. Clearly, if pregnancy increases the vitamin-D requirements they would all be in danger of developing osteomalacia. Our results show that there was no significant fall in (vitamin D) levels during pregnancy even in the group of Asian

vegetarians whose stores must have been minimal on account of their known diets.... These results argue against the idea that pregnancy increases vitamin-D requirement, and therefore predisposes to osteomalacia. Furthermore, there was nothing to suggest that the fetus suffered in any particular way.

This study appeared in the *Lancet* in late 1975. Information obtained from papers reviewed elsewhere in this book indicates that sensible vegan and vegetarian mothers do very well during all phases of pregnancy and that their offspring are also in good physical condition. Deficiencies in the diets are due usually to selection and quantity rather than quality. Personal experience with vegetarian mothers has shown them to do as well as any other mother healthwise. Large scale studies are required to enlarge our data base regarding pregnancy and vegetarianism because the total number of patients studied is still small and inadequate. In the next chapter we consider the offspring of these pregnancies and how being vegetarian has affected them.

Little Vegetarians

Various opinions are held by big people about 'little people'. With exaggeration, humanity falls into two categories regarding their attitudes towards children. The first group feels: "Here we have a baby. It is composed of a bald head and a pair of lungs." The other group, however, sees more in those young eyes:

> Happy those early days! when I
> Shined in my angel-infancy
> Before I understood this place
> Appointed for my second race,
> or taught my soul to fancy aught
> But a white celestial thought.
> —Henry Vaughan

In order to review the literature on these little creatures, we must return to the 1920s. Prior to that decade there are reports of an anecdotal nature indicating that vegetarian children suffer from unbearably good health, but the first studies, so to speak, originate somewhat later. The studies dealing specifically with children are not numerous. The reader will again find additional references to children in other chapters, such as in Hardinge's papers wherein he states that the vegan and vegetarian children in his study were in good physical condition.

In 1923, Hindhede, the Danish vegetarian scientist, produced a study of the 'Eden Settlement'. This community of 180 families in Germany lived on garden produce which was supplemented by bread, flour and margarine, milk being used only sparingly. The scientist noted, without elaboration, that the development of the children was "above the normal."

In the twenties and thirties, Dorothy Lane authored a series of studies concerned with the nutrition of children on 'vegetable diets'. One study concerned a group of children 7-15 years of age who apparently (do we doubt it?) thrived on a completely plant food diet. In 'The Nutrition of Twins on a Vegetable Diet' (1931), Lane states that: "the purpose of this experiment was to determine the result of a balanced diet of vegetable foods during pregnancy, the nursing period and infancy..."

Prior to this study she had written: "...considerable evidence had been acquired which seemed to furnish definite proof that a vegetable diet, well-balanced in the various minerals and vitamins, low in protein and fat, and comparatively high in carbohydrate, was entirely adequate for pregnancy, lactation and growth."

In the strictest sense, the mother was not a pure vegetarian, as the author allowed her to endure a "small serving" of meat once weekly (no further information provided). The entire pregnancy and lactation was carried out on the vegetable diet; the mother remained in excellent health, finally the one becoming three. Her twins weighed 6lbs.9oz and 6lbs.4oz. These infants were completely normal in all respects.

The twins were started on mother's milk, supplemented by a concoction prepared by Lane from almonds, a 'vegetable milk'. After five months, the babies' diets consisted entirely of vegetable foods. Flesh foods of any sort never touched their lips. Lane was assisted by a pediatrician who reported that at three years of age, "the sturdy physical and mental progress of these children continues to give every indication of normal development. Their great strength and endurance call for special comment." Judging by the twins I've known, I hope that the mother's endurance was also remarkable. The diet of these children consisted of wheat, barley, rice, potato, legumes and various fruits and vegetables in season.

Small and Fruitful Subjects

Lane makes a pertinent point in the paper, one which many workers today are becoming aware of:

> The conventional standards for growth in regard to weight, height and age may aid in obscuring the true facts governing general health, for over-emphasis may be placed on stature at the expense of resistance, endurance, and mentality.

At seven years of age, the twins prompted a lengthy report by the pediatrician, who discovered that—yes, you've 'guessed right'—they were in superb condition, totally vegetarian children without a blemish upon them. Lane concludes that:

> ...the apparently completely successful results of the experiments with vegetable diets with infants and children in regard to growth and health, herein reported, seem to prove that in the experiments with rats made by the Chinese physiologists, the vegetable diets were somewhat deficient...

A number of other papers during the thirties concerned children, but did not provide any earthshaking data. The following authors are listed in the bibliography for any reader who wishes to follow this up: Riestschel, Kern, Oser, Boldt, Schlutz and Langer.

Even though it is commonly known that girls aged 14-19 years are so busy giggling that they can't eat properly, Foote nevertheless studied a group of 50 children, boys and girls, who ate in a cafeteria. She concluded that these generally healthy children functioned well on a vegetarian diet, but that the girls did not receive adequate amounts of iron in their food. This statement regarding a supposed deficiency is based however, on calculated iron content from the diet and no medical studies were done to confirm this observation (nor were the girls found to be unhealthy). In this regard, there have been suggestions recently that the levels of red cells and iron considered normal in the blood streams of inhabitants of Western nations, is actually too high and possibly detrimental. One author felt that this state of 'relative polycythemia' predisposes one to bacterial infections.

In 1949, Mack concluded her series of papers in which she reported her observations on children in orphanages who were switched from high meat diets to low meat diets. Since they weren't really vegetarians we'll say no more.

One could write a book on the important story of the development of vegetable mixtures which would supply all the nutritional needs of children in the 'under-developed' nations. Since these studies touch on our topic, we will comment briefly.

The 64th Scientific Meeting of the London School of Hygiene and Tropical Medicine addressed itself to the facts known about "the comparative merits of animal and vegetable foods in nutrition." Chick presented the following summary of her findings:

> It would appear, therefore, judged by the practicability of providing a satisfactory supply of essential amino acids, that it is possible to replace animal proteins in a human diet by an appropriate combination of vegetable proteins. On these grounds alone, there would seem to be no scientific basis for the conviction, widely held, that a certain proportion of animal protein is necessary in a human diet...

Hughes studied the amino-acid intake of children in German orphanages (again), who lived on diets composed largely of bread and vegetables and compared their intakes with those children living on diets high in animal protein:

> The diets low in animal protein provided somewhat less of most of these amino-acids, but with the exception of methionine provided double the amounts required for nitrogen equilibrium in the adult.

A paper by Dean demonstrates:

> ...that we have enough evidence to show that it is possible to evolve diets containing protein exclusively from plant sources, which will rival diets containing fair amounts of animal protein.... We know there are millions of under-nourished children. We believe they could be better nourished if we used our plant resources more perfectly. We must find means of translating our belief into fact.

The belief was indeed translated into fact and, presently, there are a number of all-plant-food mixtures in use, in the poorer nations especially, which have been shown to be complete foods as regards the nutritional needs of children. What a great service for all humanity has been provided by the people involved in developing these products. Though in North America perhaps the limits on dietary choices are not economically circumscribed, in the poor areas on the globe people now have access to pure, inexpensive plant food mixtures capable of completely satisfying the nutritional needs of growing children.

The continuing problem with terminology is illustrated by the article (actually a reply to a Doctor's question) by Nagy in the *Journal of the American Medical Association* (1970). Entitled 'Teenage Vegan', the question is as follows:

> A parent is concerned about the fact that her 17-year-old daughter has recently become a vegetarian. She would like to know what harm would result and what vegetarian foods could be substituted for meat if the daughter cannot be persuaded to change her dietary views.

Nagy, from the American Medical Association Department of Foods and Nutrition, replies:

> A diet without meat may provide all the necessary nutrients for growth and good health if it is carefully planned to obtain sufficient amounts of protein from milk, eggs, cheese, and fish, as well as the plant protein in nuts and dry legumes. Vegetarians may be able to obtain all the necessary nutrition for growth and maintenance of good health, but it is somewhat difficult.

Personally, it seems to me that the average North American vegetarian would have to make a special effort to *avoid* becoming magnificently nutrited. Giving credit where it is due however, Nagy does concede that a lacto-vegetarian diet will provide sufficient nutrition to keep the motors of most vegetarians, idling.

Finally, again from the same question column, this time in 1974, a short question which, however, triggered a relatively voluminous reactive literature. "'What harm might arise from bringing up a newborn infant as a vegetarian?' asks a Doctor from Pennsylvania." The expert respondents will be very well known to those familiar with the literature on nutrition and vegetarianism, Drs. Hardinge and Mann. Having followed Dr. Mann's papers through the years, one has to admire his courage, for, knowing the unreasonable dogmatism attached to many topics in nutrition he nonetheless will state often well substantiated yet heretical thought which invariably churn up a hornets' nest of debate. His recent paper, 'Diet-Heart: End of an Era' in the Medical Intelligence column of the *New England*

Journal of Medicine (1977) stirred up such a storm; the *Journal* found that since his paper provoked "much correspondence" and while "we do not encourage rebuttal articles", one would be warranted here. Without going into the details of the above, one nonetheless gets the idea.

First, let us consider Dr. Hardinge's reply:

> ...If the food is reasonably chosen, the nutritional adequacy of the lacto-ovo-vegetarian or lacto-vegetarian diet is above question for the feeding of all age groups, including infants. Our study of adolescents raised on this diet, some of them second or third generation subjects, showed them fully comparable in development and health to adolescents raised as non-vegetarians. Allergy to cow's milk not uncommonly necessitates an alternate infant food. Probably the most common one in use is soybean 'milk'. Various brands, highly improved over the earlier products, are readily available. Pediatricians report the maintenance of an adequate nutritional state. Some parents, as a matter of preference, choose to feed their children this plant milk in place of cow's milk when the infants are not to be breast fed.
>
> A comparative evaluation of the nutritional results of feeding these two formulas to matched groups of approximately three-day-old infants was recently reported. Clinical, anthropometric, hematologic, radiologic and chemical comparisons were made. When observed, the higher values quite consistently occurred in the milk formula group. The milk-fed babies grew faster, especially in the first two weeks, and gained more weight. The authors concluded, however, that 'higher values', of course, do not necessarily mean better values. Infants fed soy milk do not experience the rapid increase in serum cholesterol that is observed in the American child fed a formula of cow's milk. One might well speculate that in the not too distant future, plant milk formulas may become the prescription of choice as a means of reducing the incidence of cardiovascular disease in the adult.

Mann replies next, somewhat provocatively and somewhat ignorantly (of previous reports to the contrary): "I think it is now possible to raise a healthy child after weaning on a vegetarian diet, but to my knowledge this has not been done, nor in my opinion should it be tried." Mann goes on to say a number of other things about the vegetarian diet which have no basis in fact. He also commented that he felt it was unethical for parents to impose their vegan practices on their children.

Before we review the last papers the reader should note that several case reports of illness in babies of supposed vegan mothers are discussed in the chapter on vitamin B_{12}.

The reader probably realizes the minor upheaval that the above comments would cause in the bosoms of those who knew better. Dr. Toppenberg of the New England Memorial Hospital wrote back:

> The comments of Dr. Mann might well leave the impression that to raise a child as a vegetarian is not done and would be nearly impossible, irresponsible and ethically incorrect. I would like to take strong exception.... To illustrate vegetarian child-raising firsthand, my three children are now the third generation of my family to have never tasted meat, and it certainly has not been detrimental to our health. My 13-year-old high school boy at 6'3" and size 14 shoes can hardly be accused of retarded physical growth, and all three children are at the top of their classes at school....

> Recent studies by Dr. John W. Berg and others at the National Cancer Institute made headlines when they linked colon cancer with beef consumption.... It would seem, then, that it would be rather overbearing for a parent to impose on a child a carnivorous diet with its implications on the three leading causes of death, heart disease, cancer, and stroke, especially since the Creator originally placed him in a garden and provided him a vegetarian diet.

Dr. Rigsby, also from the same hospital, wrote that while overseas he did well with local plant produce and suffered no ill effects. Finally, again from this hospital (sounds like a cell of vegetarians holding out there), Health Education Director, Stotz writes:

> "My wife, a school teacher, has 14 students in her class who are vegetarians. From my own personal experience, a person who is a vegetarian can be very healthy..."

The last few paragraphs may not be true scientific reports on vegetarians, but are included for the benefit of those who appreciate a good story more than a good study.

The bottom line, then, is that a balanced vegetarian diet is completely adequate for the nourishment of pregnant mothers and their subsequent offspring. There is no evidence to the contrary. Deficiency diets, whether 'vegetarian' or containing flesh-food, are capable of causing long-lasting physical and, possibly, mental problems during these two actual stages of life (pregnancy and childhood).

4

NUTRITIONAL CONCERNS

Can a Vegetarian Be Well-Nourished?

Physiology deals with the normal 'vital' processes in the human body. In this chapter, we'll be regaled with exciting tales of the pH of bile, basal metabolic rates, and other outstanding topics. They all concern some function of the human body. Related important topics, such as blood pressure, are dealt with in other chapters.

The study of basal metabolism helps one understand how the body functions, like studying your car motor when it's idling, measuring fuel consumption, heat production, etc. (the body is actually a 'chemical' engine). Earlier we mentioned that the basal metabolic rate (BMR) of vegetarians had been studied in 1913 by Benedict and Roth, who indicated that there was little difference between the BMR's of their subjects and non-vegetarians. Subsequently, in 1932, Habs studied two patients (vegetarians) and found them to be normal with metabolic rates slightly above the norm accepted at that time. Only information of limited value can be taken from this paper. Also, in 1932, Wakeham reexamined the subject:

> It was only after observing several cases of surprisingly low BMR's in vegetarian girls of normal health and intelligence that the writers of the present paper concluded that the length of the period of vegetarianism might be a factor in determining the BMR.

The authors recruited forty-three subjects and seem to have come up with some clear-cut data.

> The average BMR of twenty lifetime vegetarians was found to be 11% below the Du Bois normals.... Study of a large group of long time vegetarians indicated that a period of from 6-8 years of vegetarianism is usually required to produce this effect...It seems clear that some rather profound effect upon actual cell metabolism is indicated. Perhaps it may be tentatively suggested that the cells of the organism, confronted over a long period of time with a low supply of amino acids, gradually adjust their metabolic processes in such a way as to increase the mechanical efficiency of the body as a heat engine and thus enable the organism to carry on its normal functions with less loss of the total potential energy of the food in the form of heat.... While no physical or psychological tests were made it can be confidently stated that the subjects used in this investigation were at least up to normal averages in physical health, strength, and endurance as well as in mental intelligence and alertness.

Since it is now known that the total basal metabolism is, for all practical purposes, proportional to the body's surface area, these findings may not be so remarkable. Unfortunately, no modern studies are available which would corroborate and enlarge upon these statements.

During the thirties and forties, a number of papers and references were obtained which dealt with information concerning the physiology of vegetarians. These papers were not of high quality and perhaps even of questionable pertinence to our interests. Let me mention only one: Bronner fed patients, who had had their gall-bladders removed for various reasons, diets alternating between meat-containing diets and virtual vegetarian fare. He studied the pH of the bile which drained from the bile duct and found that it averaged 7.5 on the vegetable diets and 6.5 on the meat diets. Thus the bile was more acid on meat-containing diets; several papers during these years reveal that bile, blood, urine, etc., are generally more alkaline on vegetarian diets than meat-containing diets. The practical significance of these findings occasionally are made use of in clinical practice.

Donath et al. in 1954 produced some information from a study of a small number of Dutch vegans. They noted that their subjects were in general good health, were underweight in comparison with controls, and that their Basal Metabolic Rates were higher than the BMR's measured in control subjects when calculated on the basis of body surface area. Their hemoglobin and vitamin B-12 levels were normal but their red cells tended to be somewhat larger than average (indicating perhaps a tendency to develop anemia). We don't know how well these Dutch vegans were eating, but if they were comparable with their British counterparts, in those years, one hesitates to proclaim the nutritiousness of their diets. Hardinge's vegans, during this period of time, did much better in all categories, probably by simply taking an adequate diet.

As vegetarians are the flowers of creation, it should not be difficult, even for the sceptic, to believe intuitively that vegetarians should be blessed with goodly amounts of stamina. In Lewis's letter, 'diet and Stamina' (*British Medical Journal*, 1952), he argues against a suggestion in a daily paper that lack of meat rations produces lack of stamina and resistance in the erstwhile British population:

> Vegetarians have lived for many years and have begotten and reared healthy children who have never eaten fish, fowl, or meat. There is no evidence to show that they are less athletic or more liable to succumb to virus disease than anyone else...I should be very glad of a good scientific excuse to campaign for more meat on the grounds that our meagre ration was inimical to the health and physique of the nation. Medical men should, however, distinguish carefully between good scientific theory and wishful speculation.... At the moment all that can be said is that a meat shortage is tedious and even monotonous to a people accustomed to relying on this commodity.

This wasn't good enough for Badenoch. He responded, describing two, very ill-sounding patients, both 'vegans', who appeared to have purchased one way tickets on the Styxian Ferry. They were rescued by a return to a lacto-ovo-vegetarian diet. As far as practical information goes, none is obtainable from these histories other than the patients obviously were on deficiency diets.

Numerous studies have also been done through the years on the gastric responses, digestion, etc., to vegetable foods. These papers may be of interest to the reader but as they do not deal directly with our subject matter they will not be considered here. A sample of the genre may be found in Pathak's "'Gastric Response', Digestion and Evacuation Time of Some Vegetarian Foods".

Lest the reader think that vegetarians are capable only of generating controversy, we present the only paper found thus far dealing with the fertility of vegetarians, in this case, men in India. It reveals that:

> ...the semen of vegetarians was in no way inferior to that of non-vegetarians. More non-vegetarians than vegetarians were found in the group with the low sperm count and low sperm mobility.
>
> (Arora et al.)

Well, even though vegetarians always are "in no way inferior" in various fields, perhaps it is better to have it put this way, especially since this is a "defense manual."

In 1970, Cotes et al. wondered:

> ...if a diet containing vegetable rather than animal protein affects the physiological response to standard exercise, possibly by causing changes in skeletal muscle.

They measured lung function and the response of the heart and lungs to exercise in 14 vegan women. They found that their data did "not support the hypothesis that dietary deficiency of animal protein impairs the physiological response to submaximal exercise." Vegetarians, or vegans, anyway, thus appear to respond to exercise in a similar fashion to meat-eaters, the functions of heart and lungs not revealing any physiological inadequacy (again stating it negatively in keeping with our theme).

Our last study originated in Vietnam. Vy writes:

> In a nutrition survey of a group of Buddhist monks consuming a vegetarian diet since pre-puberty, we observed an interesting modification of the excretion of creatine and creatinine.

These latter two compounds are closely related. These Vietnamese monks showed a decreased urine creatinine excretion and an increased creatine excretion.

It will be interesting to study these excretion abnormalities further, especially to determine
whether they are related to the vegetarian diet or
to the sexual abstinence of these male adults, as
we know that creatine is normally present in the
urine of children before puberty and in women,
but not in that of normal men.

The foregoing papers provide us with odds and ends of data,
all of which suggest that a comprehensive study of the many
aspects of vegetarian physiology would be most interesting and
certainly would reveal many new and wonderous facts, no, let
us speak the truth, new and incredible facts regarding this sane
method of nutrition.

Bugs and Bile

The heading of this section sounds like the name of a quaint
English restaurant in the crusty part of town (you must have
an imagination, of course), but it actually concerns itself with a
small number of papers, dealing with physiology in general,
which have some very interesting implications. A change to the
vegetarian diet is accompanied by a variety of changes in the
functioning of the human body; only a miniscule number of
these changes have been studied and reported. The ease of
studying the bowel flora (the bacteria in stool which comprise a
large proportion by weight of the stool) has resulted in a disproportionate number of studies of bowel flora in vegetarians.
Generally, these studies are suggestive, but much further research could be done to expand our knowledge even in this one
limited area.

From about 1950 to 1956, Yano, Iinuma and Nagase authored
a series of studies which revealed strong evidence that the
change to a vegetarian type diet resulted in remarkable changes
in the ecology of the gastrointestinal tract. In sum, it was
shown that the dietary essentials, riboflavin, thiamine, and
vitamin B_6 are synthesized in much greater amounts in the
bowel (by the bacterial inhabitants) in vegetarians than in
meat-eaters, and that the absorption of these compounds from
the bowel is also increased, with the increase in absorption
greater for B_6 than for the other two compounds. Adding
cellulose to the diet of meat-eaters resulted in a similar but less
marked effect.

The reader will realize that this is important for several reasons. First, it implies that it is not unreasonable to expect similar results for other essential nutrients (already demonstrated for vitamin B_{12}). It also alerts us to the fallacy of strict adherence to the recommended daily allowances for various nutrients obtained from studies of meat-eaters. For instance, as is seen elsewhere in the book, a vegetarian's calculated intake of riboflavin may fall below the RDA, yet we would be remiss if we considered them to have a deficient diet on this basis, for the reasons stated above.

It was once thought that the upper portion of the gastrointestinal tract was sterile, but papers such as that by Moore et al., demonstrated that this was false. From small concentrations of up to 10,000 bacteria per gram in a full stomach, to about 100 billion per gram of stool in the lower bowel, each portion of the bowel has its own distinctive type of 'bugs'. Myriads of different types of bacteria have been isolated from the bowel, with new strains being discovered almost at will. The paper by Moore mentions a 10-week experiment in which 12 girls were put on a strict vegetarian diet and at the end of that time the ratios of the normally predominant bacteria in feces were relatively unchanged. The authors did note that "...the relative proportions appear to remain remarkably constant over long periods of time,"—this in regular, healthy subjects.

Further information, however, demonstrating that changes do occur, derives from Crowther's paper which showed that a type of bacteria named "*Sarcina ventriculi* was found in numbers of up to 10^8 per gram in faeces from 75 out of 106 healthy human adults living on vegetarian diets, but the organism occurred in faeces of only 2 out of 123 people living on diets containing animal products.... It is concluded that diet influences the colonization of *sarcinae* in the human intestine." The meaning of the data, at present, is unclear other than indicating that diet may have a marked effect on bowel flora.

Guineé et al., studied the possibility of transport of bacteria from animals to humans through the consumption of meat and meat products with special regard to bacteria which carry factors causing resistance to antibiotics which humans may some day require. Essentially, he found that levels of these bacteria were slightly higher in vegetarians and that this finding is unexplained (pets, etc.). As far as the authors' main concern:

...the data presented here do not permit a conclusion about the importance of foods of animal origin as a source of infection with resistant *E. coli* in man. In our material, other factors apparently prevail over a possible effect of meat and meat products.

To conclude the section dealing with bacteria alone, I reviewed the study of Drasar et al. entitled "The relation between diet and the gut microflora in man" and distilled the pertinent points from it:

The chemical nature of the diet has long been considered to exert a controlling influence on the bacterial flora of the intestine...The type of diet and frequency of feeding influences the distribution of bacteria within the small intestine of both man and animals...But, in adult man, attempts to change the colonic flora by dietary manipulation have produced equivocal results, at least as far as alterations can be detected by culture of faecal specimens...Although changes in the bacterial species and genera comprising the flora are difficult to demonstrate, changes in the metabolic activity of the flora due to changes in dietary compounds do occur.

The authors illustrate this point with a study which deals with a subject who originally could not metabolize a certain substance; by feeding it to him, his bowel flora quickly learned to degrade the substance.

Studies on bile salt metabolism have demonstrated that diet can control intestinal secretions and therefore the composition of the fluid entering the colon...The influence of diet may be indirect. The problem of demonstrating changes in bacteria flora may be partly explained by the nature of bacteriological procedures for bacterial identification. These have been developed to distinguish bacterial groups in the laboratory, not biological types in an ecological situation. Thus many of the substrates whose utilization is important in bacterial identification may be without significance in the bio-economics of bacterial growth in the intestine.

In other words, a new approach to this question may be required before meaningful results are obtained.

We will now, in order to aid in the digestion of a few papers, simplify bile acid metabolism almost beyond belief. From cholesterol, the body manufactures primary bile acids and from the latter the secondary bile acids are made. Anything deeper than this is beyond our purview. Deoxycholic acid, a secondary bile acid formed in the bowel by bacteria (from cholic acid, a primary bile acid) has, under certain conditions, been shown to be oncogenic (cancer causing). Interestingly, (as an aside) when a doctor is the cause of a patient's medical problem we say the illness is 'iatrogenic'. This word however means, if we're to be consistent, 'to generate doctors'. Thus medical schools may be iatrogenic (in more ways than one) but the only medical condition that is iatrogenic appears to be a pregnancy in a future doctor's mother. Apparently, the term 'iatral' should be used as in 'iatral illness'. Perhaps this point will one day be clarified.

As we were saying, a number of bile acids appear to be oncogenic because bacteria in the large bowel convert them into cancer-causing compounds. The paper by Aries et al. found a much lower percentage of bacteria from the large bowel of strict vegetarians had the ability to convert bile acids to these dangerous compounds, than the bacteria found in meat-eaters. They also found that there are lesser amounts of bile acids excreted in strict vegetarians as compared with meat-eaters. The excretion of bile acids is usually proportional to the dietary fat intake. Considering these two findings together, the authors thought that:

> ...such reactions (conversion to cancer causing substances) would be more likely to occur in the intestine of people on a mixed diet since their gut bacteria are more active against bile acids, and the reaction could be more important in these people since the substrate (bile acids) concentration in their intestine is higher.

Pomare and Heaton showed in 1973 that by adding dietary fibre to the diet the bacterial metabolism of bile salts is also changed. The fibre they used was bran. The theory again, is that large bowel bacteria breakdown bile acids into dangerous compounds which may cause bowel cancer. These workers found that dietary fibre reduced the chances of this 'breakdown' taking place.

Finally, we note a study by Hepner (1975) in which he found that bile acid metabolism is *fundamentally* altered in vegetarians, again theoretically in a direction which might protect against large bowel cancers. Hepner found that vegetarians had altered bile acid metabolism such that when compared with meat-eaters, in technical terms, the daily fractional turnover rate of cholic acid was significantly smaller, the deoxycholic acid pool size was significantly smaller, while there was no difference in the synthesis rate of the primary bile acids in the two groups.

Deoxycholic acid is thought to be one of the substances which *can be* converted by bacteria in the bowel to a cancer causing agent. Hepner goes on to say, that while it had been thought that lack of dietary fibre in the meat-eating population produced the right conditions for cancer causing agents to be formed in the bowel, his study suggests that the effect of meat *per se* requires further investigation. The professional reader will find this paper to be of interest.

Even prior to entering medical school, I was aware of the intimate relationship between food and bowels. "A good reliable set of bowels is worth more to a man than any quantity of brains." (Henry Wheeler Shaw)

Howard Spiro, the author of one of the most readable textbooks I've come across (*Gastroenterology*), had an article in the *New England Journal of Medicine* in 1975, which, although it mentions vegetarianism only peripherally, is worthy of a few quotes:

> Giving diets often brings out the priest in an otherwise phlegmatic physician. Food habits, after all, have been one of the ways in which groups have separated themselves from other peoples. One religion chews what another culture eschews...Today high fibre diets are popular... Burkitt has been foremost in bringing attention back to a possible connection between diet, constipation, and many physical disorders. He might have been regarded as only an eccentric dabbling in the past if he had not already observed and described African lymphoma. Burkitt observed that African blacks had many and copious bowel movements and little colon cancer...Others took up the hypothesis, now to teach the physician the evils of the low fibre diet, how bacteria flourish-

ing in the colon of meat-eaters turn otherwise un-offending bile salts into carcinogens, how, like a sponge, fibre soaks up cholesterol to clean coronary vessels as it scrubs the colon—and more!... Many colleges now have vegetarian menus and dining areas; more books on vegetarianism are appearing in the popular press; and so I suppose that vegetarianism is on the increase. Now that the parent is on a high fibre diet to prevent diverticular disease and colon cancer and now that his child is a vegetarian, for more doctrinaire reasons, they can meet in one great if gassy festival of love over cauliflower, broccoli, and carrots. Spinach, which stood for the authority of the parents and divided the generations in the 1920s, now symbolizes their unity...

The results of all these studies are quite interesting, both for their specific findings and for merely hinting at the fact that there appear to be some very fundamental differences in people which are due to their diets alone and that these differences may have a strong bearing on questions of health. Would you believe that I was so excited by some of these findings that I awoke my wife at two a.m. just to explain them to her. She was less than pleased saying (sweetly, of course), "Well, you may possibly be low in bile but you certainly have your gall!"

Vegetarianism and Protein

Is it the lack of protein in the diet which transforms vegetarians into small, shrivelled creatures resembling tree frogs with stomach trouble? The common misperception of protein or Vitamin B_{12} problems in vegetarianism are not limited to the lay person, but often medical and other professionals are similarly misled. In the movie "Casablanca" when there is a problem, the police chief orders, "Round up the usual suspects!" and in our case, whatever the problem, it's usually protein that's seen as the culprit. We're not speaking of cases of malnutrition here, but simply of the average, happy-go-lucky vegetarian whose diet has been for years considered inadequate on the basis of its protein content. Times have changed. "Recent advances in our understanding of protein requirements free us from dependence on animal protein and allows us to concentrate on ways of most efficiently and economically meeting man's need. The bulk of present and future needs will be met by conventional plant proteins." Thus spake Scrimshaw.

Since the mid-1940s the ideas of man's nutritional requirements for protein, both amounts and sources, have changed gradually but markedly. Register writes:

> A number of the very early studies used the rat growth method for evaluating the quality of single proteins. By this method the quality of plant proteins was generally undervalued. However, the concept of mutual supplementation evolved. As pointed out in the *Lancet* (2:956, 1959): Formerly vegetable proteins were classified as second-class and regarded as inferior to first-class proteins of animal origin; but this distinction has now been generally discarded. Certainly some vegetable proteins, if fed as the *sole* source of protein, are of relatively low value for promoting growth; but many field trials have shown that the proteins provided by suitable mixtures of vegetable origin enable children to grow as well as children provided with milk and other animal proteins."

This was discussed briefly in the chapter on children. But Bressani and Behar have also commented:

> From a nutritional point of view, animal or vegetable proteins should not be differentiated. It is known today that the relative concentration of the amino acids, particularly the essential ones, is the most important factor determining the biological value of a protein...By combining different proteins in appropriate ways, vegetable proteins cannot be distinguished nutritionally from those of animal origin. The amino acids and not the proteins should be considered as the nutritional units.

Jenkins and all the other scientists writing in the field recently, agree.

> The distinction between protein types should be disregarded...There is no problem in receiving an adequate protein intake from the vegetarian diet. In fact, intakes of amino acids have been found to range from twice to many times greater than the essential amino acid requirements. Hegsted, et al., reported that "it is difficult to obtain a mixed

vegetable diet which will produce an appreciable loss of body protein without resorting to high levels of sugar, jams and jellies and other essentially protein-free food...While protein receives the greatest attention in the vegetarian literature it is also extremely important to consider the total calories consumed.

Many of the reports from various nations which are primarily vegetarian, discuss diseases which are due, not to the vegetarian fare per se, but to a major deficit of calories and/or to the reliance on only one inadequate type of vegetable, such as cassava root (which, incidentally, contains near toxic levels of cyanide). Parasitic diseases also play an important role as causative factors in malnutrition.

Earlier in the section on nutrition, protein and amino acids were briefly discussed and the lay reader may find it helpful to quickly review that material as well as the just-quoted report by Bressani and Behar. The human body doesn't need protein as such but it does need eight essential amino acids (adult). These will be obtained from ingested protein foods which can vary in amino acid pattern. And so the concept of complementary plant foods evolved.

Just one example of a dietary combination that supplies "perfect protein" is the combination of wheat based food with beans. Wheat is a good source of protein; it tends to be low in lysine (an essential amino acid) and high in methionine (another essential amino acid). The amino acid pattern in beans shows somewhat lower methionine values and higher lysine values. Taken together, beans and wheat can 'supplement' each other. The suggested ratio is 70/30 (wheat/legume). This concept is discussed in more detail in various other books. The extend to which these amino acid 'deficiencies' might, in actuality, cause a problem is unknown (except for some foods which have little or *no* amounts of some amino acids, but this is rare).

Many studies, such as those done of the Otami natives in Mexico, Hunzas in Asia and others, reveal that those who are unsophisticated in dietary knowledge often seem to have naturally evolved diets based on foods that make use of this type of 'complementation' in protein sources. Frequent demonstrations of the fact that humanity does not require any animal protein to live a normal life abound. There is not one medical condition in existence that requires a meat-containing diet to aid in restoring the body's health. If your Doctor has told you that "such and such-itis" requires a pound of beef daily in order to effect a cure, just mail him or her to me in a stamped, self-addressed box and I'll convince them otherwise.

The evidence for these statements, besides that shown by the many healthy vegetarians worldwide, comes from studies such as those by Hardinge in which vegetarians who were found to be in good health ingested approximately 70-80 grams of protein daily and suffered not at all from protein or amino-acid deficiencies. Vegans, who use no animal protein, and children fed on plant food mixtures as a source of protein do extremely well.

Needs for various essential amino acids vary in relationship to pregnancy, age, physical activity, and other such factors. The lowest intake of protein I've been able to find in studies of healthy vegetarians was 10 grams (one-third ounce) daily. Kempner reports that his experimental subjects taking 20 grams of protein daily, were in good health and maintained themselves in a state of nitrogen balance, indicating that their nutritional needs were being satisfied at this level.

The studies of vegetarians in relation to protein demonstrate that the sane North American vegetarian's protein needs are fulfilled completely by the diet in all stages of life. The studies done thus far, however, have been of the nature of gathering a group of vegans or vegetarians, examining their diets and calculating the amounts of amino acids ingested. Their health is checked out and then the appropriate conclusions drawn. The next step required is to study the actual metabolism of protein in particular vegans and vegetarians to discover if their requirements for various amino acids are altered in any way. We know they obtain adequate amounts when taking a good diet but it would be interesting if, for example, a certain essential amino acid was found to be essential only in those who eat meat. Even such fanciful speculation aside, it is clear from a scientific viewpoint that much more research must be done, again not to discover if vegetarians or vegans can live on plant protein adequately (for this is no longer debatable) but rather to ascertain the basic evidence of vegetarian amino acid metabolism and requirements.

Legumes, nuts, cereals, and even fruits supply essential amino acids; obtaining the correct quantity is a pleasurable pastime for most. A number of companies, following the lead of workers at Loma Linda University, have produced endless varieties of "meat analogs", tasty foods derived from vegetable protein (mainly, or often, from the star of the bean world, the soybean) textured and shaped into products resembling the commonly used meat products. You can buy wieners, steaks, burgers, etc., all formed of vegetable protein. Initially this idea upset me (as a purist) but now, as the world moves towards a meat-free diet, it seems possible that these various tasty deceptions might actually ease the discomfort many meat-eaters feel on 'conversion'.

Papers on vegetarian diets, the food types, their preparation and so on, are also found in the medical literature. Many interesting facts are noted but these papers do not fit in with the main body of information being presented in this book. The articles are generally written in non-medical terms and will be of interest to many readers. (Gilson, Zolber, Jenkins, Raper and Hill, Register and Sonnenburg, Williams, and others have contributed to this literature.) The Seventh Day Adventists, who have been conspicuous in the medical fields relating to nutrition and vegetarianism, operate hospitals in which the standard fare for patients and staff alike consists of nutritionally balanced vegetarian cuisine.

Meat-eaters converting to vegetarianism have several options open to them. Those changing for philosophical or religious reasons often go "cold-turkey" (excuse me). Others try to cut down on meat in the diet, increasing the plant protein daily until they finally emerge triumphantly as true vegetarians. When following the latter course of action, the best sign indicating that you are on the vegetarian threshold and that meat should be stopped completely, is waking-up in the morning, singing and feeling that it's a great day to be alive.

Millions of vegetarians attest to the protein adequacy of their diet both verbally and physically, and the scientific literature supports completely the contention that plant foods can be the sole source of mankind's nutritional needs, especially with regard to the essential amino-acids. Many physicians are or have become vegetarians. Reports such as that by Grosse-Brockhoff on a young, 'strict' vegetarian doctor, confirm that even physicians are able to survive on a completely plant food diet, at no risk to their health.

Vegans and Vitamin B $_{12}$
[or, Bread, Potatoes and Candy will do you in!]

Of the three Great Mysteries of the Universe, only one is familiar to this writer and will be discussed in this book. This third Great Mystery—the relationship between Vitamin B $_{12}$ and vegans—is the topic of this chapter. Earlier it was clearly shown that the 'standard' vegetarian enjoys a diet which supplies him or her with all the known nutritional requirements, often much more than required. There is no scientific question about the nutritional status of these folks. The trusty vegan, on the other hand, by eliminating *all* foods from animal sources, has carried us one step further. As long as we must eat to survive, and as long as we must kill to eat (be it animal or plant), then, the vegan argues we must do the least harm possible, taking for our food the plant life which has lower qualities of consciousness than the higher forms of animal life. Presently, the only problem seriously raised regarding the 'all-plant-food-diet' relates to the possible nutritional deficiency of Vitamin B $_{12}$ in *vegans*, because of supposedly low amounts in the food ingested. The question of protein requirements on this diet (as noted in the last section) are no longer seriously entertained, since many workers have shown that the human body's needs are more than adequately met (see Dean, McCance, and others). Aware of the evidence that the lacto-vegetarian need 'fear no evil' regarding the adequacy of his or her diet, I still felt impelled to investigate the problem stated above, for it appears innately true that man must be following his highest instincts when dining upon plant life alone and, therefore, whatever problems had arisen would in turn be resolved by diligent inquiry. There is in fact a good deal of uncertainty in the literature. The sporadic case studies of dubious quality (as we shall see), are not encouraging. Perhaps we should acquiesce—

> "Oh! Let us never, never doubt
> What nobody is sure about."
> —Hillaire Belloc, *Cautionary Verses*

but in view of the fact that this is in a sense, a defense manual, entering the fray is much more apropos. Vegans are, at present, few in number and represent a minority of the vegetarian population. However, the information obtained from them does have very important implications. Furthermore, let it not be said that the studies to be reviewed were subjected to a biased analysis, for this writer's mind was wide open (not gaping, however) on the topic. If the reader only wishes to know the conclusions reached, turn to the summary at the end of the chapter, but if you enjoy a digression, please continue reading.

Prior to 1926, informing a patient that he was suffering from pernicious anemia, was tantamount to passing a death sentence upon him. Fortunately, in that year, Minot and Murphy discovered that by feeding these patients heaps of liver or concentrates of liver, they could be literally snatched from the jaws of death and returned to leading fairly normal lives. Whatever was the cause of this atrophy of the stomach lining and the attendant fatal consequences such as anemia, it certainly responded to the scientists' treatment. Research, stimulated by this remarkable finding, eventually elicited the following story. There appeared to be a factor in food called 'extrinsic factor' which when combined with a factor secreted by the gastric (stomach) lining, terming 'intrinsic factor,' was absorbed by the gut into the body and prevented the onset of the fatal process which resulted from a deficiency of the combination. Extrinsic factor turned out to be Vitamin B_{12}, thusly named because the substance behaved like a B-vitamin and B_{11} was already taken with another, now not so important, substance. The process by which B_{12} is absorbed is unique amongst the nutritional substances, for none of the others require a product secreted by the body to aid their absorption.

Although much is known of the function of the B_{12} molecule in bacteria, I don't think I would be inviting a flood of letters from biochemists and other knowledgeable persons, if I stated that the actual function of B_{12} in the human body is, as yet, not clearly defined. A marked deficiency of this substance results in the malfunctioning of a great number of cells in the body, presumably by interfering with DNA (genetic material) synthesis. There are three main conditions associated with B_{12} deficiency in the human; nervous lesions, mental disorders and megaloblastic anemia, this latter condition characterized by an anemia with the blood cells being larger than normal.

Dorothy Hodgkin won a Nobel Prize for determining the structure of Vitamin B_{12}. This unique molecule, consisting of hundreds of atoms bonded together forming a structure like a majestic intergalactic spacecraft, is related in several ways to both hemoglobin and chlorophyll. The metabolically active molecule is thought to take several forms. The subject, chemically, is complex and the terminology is mind-bending; in fact, I think that more nervous system damage has been done to humans who have tried to understand the chemistry of B_{12} than will probably occur due to a deficiency of the molecule in the diet of vegans. Let's briefly touch on the physiology involved.

It has been determined, after a great deal of study (and with due regard to the phases of the moon), that the average meat-eating human being requires roughly 2.5 micrograms of B_{12} by mouth daily, a very tiny amount. Some studies show as little as 0.5 *micro*grams are required whereas several indicate that larger amounts are required to maintain good health. No studies dealing with the vegan or vegetarian and their basic requirements have apparently been conducted thus far.

During digestion, B_{12} is released from food and forms a complex with 'intrinsic factor' which is secreted by the parietal cells of the stomach lining. This complex travels down the small intestine to the distant portion (the ileum), where it is captured by specific receptor molecules located on the gut lining which seem to relish B_{12} and nothing else! Only 1.5 micrograms of B_{12} can be absorbed at one particular time by the intrinsic factor mechanism. This mechanism is termed an 'active' mechanism as opposed to a 'passive' mechanism which also exists for B_{12}. The latter operates whenever *large* amounts of B_{12} are ingested orally, perhaps hundreds or even thousands of times the normal intake, and the vitamin simply forces its way into the body due to the overwhelming quantity.

When the B_{12} enters the blood stream it is bound to a protein transporter (transcobalamin II). The transport protein carries the molecules to the many growing cells in the body which absorb the substance and allow it to perform its somewhat mysterious functions. Any B_{12} which might remain in circulation after eight hours or so is bound to another protein, transcolbalamin I, whose function is relatively unknown. The average human being has stores in the liver of about 2-4 milligrams (again a very small amount) which, however, will last for several years if, for some reason, the supply of B_{12} to the bloodstream should cease.

It has been stated, that in the early research on Vitamin B_{12}, it took one ton of liver to produce 20 milligrams of B_{12} crystal. In order to provide an illustration of the small amount of B_{12} *stores* that the average human contains, I took a spare moment one day to drop into the lab of the small hospital near my clinic. Finding that common objects such as pennies and dimes were much too heavy (weighing grams rather than milligrams or thousandths of grams) I switched to weighing some dead Box Elder bugs which had collected in a hidden corner of the lab. (Perhaps, like elephants, Box Elder bugs have a secret place where they go to die.) Nonetheless, it turns out that the weight of one of these tiny creatures equals roughly the amount of B_{12} that a human being needs for 4-5 years of life. It also turns out that lab directors are not thrilled to find outsiders using delicate weigh scales for extraordinary or unofficial purposes.

Bile provides the main route of excretion of B_{12} from the body. With a normally operating intrinsic factor mechanism, two-thirds to three-quarters of the biliary B_{12} is reabsorbed in the ileum and is thus again made available to the body. One might speculate that vegans, many of whom have fairly high levels of B_{12} in the blood after 20-30 years or more on the diet, could have achieved this in several ways; increasing the above noted circulation of the molecule between liver and gut, decreasing the excretion and/or having a modified bowel flora which enables increased gut synthesis and absorption.

Where do we obtain Vitamin B_{12}? The whole 'problem' revolves around the fact at B_{12} is manufactured *only* by certain bacteria, a small number of molds, and a few other micro-organisms and therefore any B_{12} in a natural source ultimately can be traced back to these tiny forms of life. Thus far, any evidence of B_{12} in plant material has eventually been shown to originate in bacteria and molds inadvertently assayed along with the plant substance. All B_{12} in liver and other meats originates with micro-organisms. The human body doesn't appear to manufacture its own directly (it strikes me as a very good idea to have this ability, but for some reason...).

Smith states:

> The presence of B_{12}-producing organisms in their natural habitats leads to very low concentrations in soil, ponds, and even the sea. Thus primitive communities may acquire significant intakes from domestic water supplies.

Earlier in the same paper (this may have some bearing on the paper by Halsted in 1960, reviewed later), Smith writes:

> Vitamin B_{12} is of special concern to vegans. Alone among the vitamins and accessory food factors, it is for all practical purposes missing from a strict vegan diet. This is the rock of truth upon which founders the argument put forward by some vegans that the vegan diet is natural, ordained, and fully adequate for man. It is an ironical fact that man living in a truly natural state like the animals, uninhibited by civilised man's excessive regard for cleanliness and hygiene, would probably get by. Thus rhesus monkeys on a fruitarian diet in hygienic captivity sometimes suffer from B12 deficiency, though they are healthy in the wild;...

Furthermore:

> Many of the bacteria that inhabit the lower intestinal tract are producers of vitamin B_{12}, but in most species this production occurs below the region from which absorption occurs, so that no direct benefit accrues from this source...A curious situation prevails in some vegans after many years on the diet. As reserves accumulated on previous dietary regimes are used up the serum levels fall, but tend to stabilize around 100 ug/ml., just about on the danger-line, though these individuals appear to enjoy excellent health. If they are strict vegans taking no B_{12} supplements, it is a puzzle where the vitamin comes from to maintain this level, low though it is. It has been suggested that their diet may encourage the invasion of the normally sterile upper intestine and even the stomach by B_{12} producing micro-organisms... alternatively, they may have acquired the ability to absorb from the lower levels of the digestive tract.

Finally, a note should be made of folic acid, whose dietary deficiency can result in an anemia resembling that of B_{12} deficiency. If this substance, which is plentiful in an average vegan diet, is deficient for some reason, the effects become apparent after only a few months, as opposed to years as in the case of B_{12}.

Any reader who has pursued the matter thus far will probably realize that many reasons could result in a person becoming B$_{12}$ deficient. The major factors involved are listed below:

1. *Decreased intake*—Harrison's textbook *Principles of Internal Medicine* (along with most medical and nutritional texts) puts 'Vegetarianism' under this subheading. Now regarding vegetarianism—both you and I know that it doesn't belong here and if we weren't so anemic, our blood would be boiling. That is not to say, however, that some people definitely do become deficient solely because of a *poor* diet.

2. *Malabsorption*—factors which can cause B$_{12}$ to be improperly absorbed.
   a) Relative lack of intrinsic factor
      —pernicious anemia
      —various types of surgery on the stomach because of ulcers, cancer, etc., remove the cells which produce intrinsic factor.
   b) Problems with the ileum, the site of absorption in the small bowel
      —tropical and non-tropical sprues
      —myriads of other small bowel diseases
      —B$_{12}$ recepter defect (rare)
   c) Drugs—various types; PAS, colchicine, neomycin—all, in different ways, impair B$_{12}$ absorption.
   d) Competition for the molecule—bacteria in the bowel (blindloop syndrome); fish tapeworm.

This latter agent, the fish tapeworm, is an interesting fellow. Higher rates of B$_{12}$ deficiency in Scandinavians were finally traced to the tapeworms' appetite for this molecule. It's a sign of the times, as one author now notes, that due to the increasing amounts of pollution, the fish are dying off and subsequently there is less tapeworm and so less B$_{12}$ deficiency due to the parasite.

Deficiency of folic acid leading to fairly comparable blood problems can be traced in a similar fashion. Drugs, excessive cooking of food (B$_{12}$ destroyed significantly also), sprues, increased requirements due to pregnancy, birth control pills, and alcohol can all lead to this clinical deficiency state. By now, even the most enterprising digressor will have the feeling that this has really become too thin to plow, yet is too thick to chew. What is all this going to prove? Well, just this: it should be apparent that the causes of the various symptoms of B_{12} deficiency are legion and that to say (as is often done), that if a vegan has a vitamin B_{12} problem, then, ipso facto the problem is due to a lack of B_{12} in the diet, is, without adequate investigation, a completely invalid conclusion. Stating that a vegan, or anyone else for that matter, if B_{12} deficient *solely* on the basis of dietary insufficiency is a very difficult contention to scientifically substantiate. None of the papers reviewed (to let the cat out of the bag) has done this unequivocally, even though most have claims to the contrary. Zealots amongst us might feel that no matter how diligently the case is pursued, the requirements needed to substantiate the diagnosis can simply be made stricter; but this is not the case, for the deficiencies in the various papers (from a scientific point of view) are not subtle and little fanaticism is required to malign their conclusions.

Review of the Evidence

'Vitamin B_{12} Deficiency in a Vegan' is a popular title for these case histories, the article usually recording the story of some poor soul who lived solely upon candies and potatoes ('for religious reasons') or another variant, perhaps even more religious, subsisting on tomatoes for breakfast, tomatoes for dinner and tomatoes for supper. As soon as these dietary explorers run into medical problems, they become famous, published as above, and who can really contest the fact that they certainly abstained from using all animal products in their diets? This type of case is not adequate for our purposes for obvious reasons. Their deficiencies are more debilitating than that of B_{12}.

Another major and related problem exists with the large percentage of published studies that do not include *any* dietary investigation at all, simply stating that the subject refrained from animal products but not hinting at what the subject actually did eat. From a medical point of view this constitutes a no-no which again renders the whole case history practically meaningless.

Early reports, dating to the 1950s, are the ones most often quoted and brandished about as indicating deficiencies in the vegan diet. The earliest ones are not helpful, as serum levels for

B_{12} were not done. In 1955, Wokes studied British vegans (who had been in existence for about ten years by that time) and compared them with American vegans (from Hardinge's studies which have been reviewed under separate heading) and Dutch vegans (studies of Donath, de Wijn and others). He found that whereas no clinical deficiency symptoms had been observed among the American vegans and few amongst the Dutch, the British vegans had a fairly high incidence of complaints ranging from sore mouths and tongues, to menstrual disturbances and back pains. He studied the levels of B_{12} and found them to be lower in the vegans than in the average population but:

> ...no correlation was established between the serum vitamin B_{12} levels and any of the other blood values measured...As this investigation is concerned primarily with vitamin B_{12} we have not undertaken the detailed investigation of all the nutrients in the diets of all the vegans, nor endeavoured to determine their status in regard to any vitamin except B_{12}.

I personally wonder what the total picture might have revealed; I suspect something approaching a general malnutrition.

American vegans had a higher rate of protein intake (10.4%) when compared with the British (7%) and this may have accounted for some of the differences in their respective physical conditions.

Wokes was interested in the vegans as a model for parts of the world where people of necessity must eat diets low in animal protein. He notes in his 1956 paper, his puzzlement at the fact that many vegans had normal or low-normal B_{12} levels in spite of a diet which theoretically was devoid of B_{12}. He also remarks on the fact that many seemed healthy while cataloging the variour ills that had befallen some. Possible reasons for the problems the British vegans at that time experienced were reviewed:

> Pulses contain much less methionine than cereals and British vegans consuming large amounts of pulses may well have experienced methionine deficiency. (Methionine is one of the essential amino acids.)

(For the reader's edification, or ingestion for that matter, pulses are edible seeds of peas, beans, lentils or any member of the legume family.)

At about this time it became fashionable to state that vegans and vegetarians suffered a Vitamin B$_{12}$ *deficiency* simply on the basis of their generally lower than 'average' serum levels of B$_{12}$. This makes as much sense as saying meat-eaters suffered in a significant fashion, simply because of their higher levels of B$_{12}$. Once 'norms' had been established using the general population it was proper to feel a deficiency existed if low values occurred in these blood tests. Mollin (1976) produced a comprehensive paper on the significance of the serum B$_{12}$ level and this paper explains many of the problems faced in accurately measuring this compound and understanding its (the serum levels) meaning. This level cannot be taken in isolation but must be correlated with the clinical findings.

In the early sixties Guggenheim studied the diets in a vegan kibbutz in Israel and found that the members met or exceeded all the recommended amounts of nutrients except for riboflavin. This doesn't mean that they were deficient but only that their dietary *intake* was less than recommended for meat-eaters. As we noted earlier, Yano from Tokyo, reported:

> Iinuma has found in human experiments that riboflavin synthesis is markedly greater with a vegetable diet than with a meat diet and Nagase demonstrated in human experiments that the effect was chiefly due to cellulose...Similar findings were likewise observed by Nagase with thiamine.

Yano found the same effects occurring when he studied vitamin B$_6$. This is *very* interesting and tends to support our contention that vegans and vegetarians may have different metabolisms and different physiologies (different nutritional requirements) than the lowly meat-eaters.

In 1960, Bourne and Oleesky reviewed the literature on Vitamin B$_{12}$ dietary deficiency, much as we've done here. They described their criteria for deciding whether a case of B$_{12}$ deficiency was due *solely* to dietary deficiency rather than being secondary to some other cause such as bowel disease. They present a case but, unfortunately, it doesn't even meet their own criteria, since they recommend but did not obtain a serum B$_{12}$ level from their patient. Amongst the cases that meet their approval as true vitamin deficiencies on a dietary basis is that of Harrison (1956), which upon reading we discover the following: the subject is a 77-year-old lady who, "since 1943 had existed on a diet of bread, margarine, tea and potatoes." Amongst her other physical problems was a gastro-enterostomy (gastrointestinal surgery), performed many years previously, which again rules out her case according to the criteria of Bourne and Oleesky.

As seems customary, a subsequent issue of the *British Medical Journal* contained a note from Jeffs, on Bourne and Oleesky's report:

> The challenging problem is that of why some vegans do not develop signs of a lack of this vitamin. I have in mind the case of a girl who is a life vegan, a true human herbivore in fact. From birth the only animal food of any kind which she has had was her own mother's milk, from which she received nourishment for the first 2 years and 8 months of her life. The child is normally developed physically and mentally and has managed to avoid all the common infections of childhood.

The following authors all attempted to describe Vitamin B 12 deficiencies in vegans or vegetarians (due solely to dietary insufficiency). All were judged wanting for various important reasons, such as the use of drugs, habitual blood donation, gastrointestinal surgery etc.: Schlosser, Smith, Harrison, Pollycove, Bourne, Hines, Riley, Connor, Ledbetter, Verjaal, Gleeson, Green, and among others. Technically most of these papers are more deficient than the diets of their case studies.

Again in the journals, this time in the *Lancet*, a few cages are rattled. Apparently Dr. Haler wrote a note to the *'Times'* implicating a vegan diet as the cause of death in an oldtimer. This time Ellis responded (perhaps only a medical professional can see the hackles that would be raised by this seemingly innocuous statement):

> Dr. D. Haler's recently reported opinion that the vegan diet is a 'potential killer' suffers from the absence of substantiating clinical data. To suggest that it is a 'grossly deficient diet' shows ignorance of available knowledge about the vegan diet.... We should like to ask Dr. Haler on what grounds he bases his evidence that this case is the

third recent death attributable to the vegan diet. It is known that there are large numbers of old people who for financial reasons subsist mainly on 'tea and buns' and such a diet can lead to serious deficiencies and malnutrition. It is obvious that one could not classify this group as vegans.

Dr. Haler replies sweetly:

Had Dr. Ellis and his colleagues taken the trouble to communicate with me personally I could have relieved their minds of many of the problems which they have now ventilated...If she had been a vegan she would have had, I have no doubt, a dietetic supplement which turns this peculiar diet into one which is not necessarily always lethal. I fully accept that such cults must be permitted, or tolerated...As for the suggestion in the last but one paragraph of Dr. Ellis and his colleagues' letter that the old lady did not die from her stupid dietetic habits and, in fact, might have been preserved, I can only say that this is ludicrous...I know that there are large numbers of old people who subsist mainly on 'tea and buns': may I point out that this diet is not a vegan diet, because buns should be made with milk.

Oh! what passion can (nutrition) not raise and quell?

At this point it appears quite safe to say that where the vegan takes a variety of good quality foods such as those available to the average North American, there is no evidence that he or she or their children will suffer because of their diet and if they wish to supplement their diets with Vitamin B_{12} (the supplements are entirely non-animal products, by the way), there should be no cause for complaint by anyone.

Moving on to some other studies concerning the vegan and vegetarian way of life, I now introduce the disappearing boy. In the early part of this century, Sir Leonard Hill discovered a boy "whose parents, people of culture, are strict and ardent vegetarians." The child's life is presented in detail. He appears to be an average super-human vegetarian. He walks 5 miles to church every morning before breakfast. He "is in fine form, full of life and energy, and getting stronger and tougher rapidly. Anybody who likes could come and observe there is no deception; only the workings of God's laws of nature in a clean young organism..." Sir Leonard's study revealed that the boy consumed oxygen at the rate of 215 cc/min and that his daily dietary intake was 800 calories. Inexplicably, the article concludes with a comparison of super-boy and the chimps in the local zoo.

Dr. Rabinowitch of the Montreal General Hospital, wrinkled his brow, sharpened his pencil and discovered that on the basis of the information provided and taking into consideration the known laws of thermodynamics and human physiology, this child had a deficit of 465 calories daily. "In one year, therefore, this boy should lose about 40 lbs. Since he weighs 59 lbs., he should disappear completely in less than two years." I was going to mention that Rabinowitch certainly never argued that wonder-boy wasn't healthy and only contested the metabolic measurements provided, but on the other hand, has anyone ever heard of this child since?

Vegans and vegetarians have been found to be healthy, certainly not suffering symptoms of B_{12} deficiency when their diet is varied and of good quality. Numerous studies provide this information. Dhopeshwarkar (1956) found low B_{12} levels in his vegetarian subject (he calls it 'a lack') and suggests "that the lack of vitamin B_{12} in the vegetarians did not result in any clinical evidence of deficiency of this vitamin despite the fact that the level in the vegetarians was so much lower than in the meat-eaters."

Banerjee (1960) reaches a similar conclusion. Halsted in 1960 reported on his studies of Iranian villagers who were virtual vegans and found that their B_{12} levels did not differ from 'normal' levels noted in their compatriots (meat-eaters). This paper is especially interesting in light of the previously mentioned comments by Smith that 'natural' living might enable vegans to obtain significant amounts of B_{12} from their immediate environment.

Satoskar and others, in several papers published through the years, showed that "in spite of considerably lower serum vitamin B_{12} values, the lacto-vegetarians have no apparent signs or symptoms of vitamin B_{12} deficiency..." Our heroes were also shown to have generally lower serum cholesterol levels and, surprisingly, lower folic acid levels. This latter finding is rarely if ever noted in any of the subsequent papers, the folic acid levels usually are elevated in vegans and vegetarians when compared with meat-eaters, as they obtain this substance in abundance from plant foods.

Ellis, whose name pops up everywhere in this literature, equates low serum B_{12} levels with 'deficiency' even as late as the 1970s. We've already commented on this and validly so I believe. In his paper in the *American Journal of Clinical Nutrition* (1970), Ellis notes that his subjects, who were vegans, were lighter in weight than omnivores, were in equally as good health, had lower serum B_{12} levels and lower cholesterol levels (males only), had higher folic acid levels and a few had higher serum bilirubin levels, than the control omnivores. Significantly for the general reader, Ellis notes, "There were no abnormal symptoms or signs of definite significance in the vegans in the present study relating to an inadequate nutritional status." Actually a significant number of the meat-eating control subjects suffered raised blood urea levels of obscure etiology.

Electroencephalograms and Vegans

Things were progressing along so nicely when several studies from the early '60s onward (Smith, Ellis, Kurtha), revealed 'abnormal' brain-wave tracings in a number of vegans. Summarizing all the findings to date: unlike the abnormal traces in patients with pernicious anemia and B_{12} deficiency, the abnormalities in the vegans were unaffected by B_{12} injections. Furthermore, these abnormalities were not associated with any mental or other health problems and are at present unexplained. It should be noted that the word 'abnormality' means simply (loosely), "not usually found in the norm," in this case, the meat-eater. Vegetarians did not seem to have the same type of changes as were found in the vegans.

If you are worried or if you should be accused of being mad by reason of becoming a vegetarian, take some comfort from Jathar's paper in which he states it is "difficult to accept any relationship between low serum vitamin B_{12} levels and functional psychosis where one is dealing with a lacto-vegetarian population..." (at least in India).

A number of interesting findings were revealed by McKenzie in his 1970 paper, 'Profile on Vegans'. "Vegans living in Britain are, to a large extent, separated off from the rest of society." They tended to use natural cures or treatments for minor medical complaints, visiting the medical practitioner far less often than average. Not only did the British vegans tend to be isolated from the general society, they remained isolated from each other for the most part. Many readers would enjoy reading this paper in its entirety. Hopefully, when the whole world is vegan, the above will no longer be a problem, although the casual observer will have noted that meat-eaters don't always excel in social intercourse either.

Ellis (1967) reviewed several other authors' papers and concluded:

> These authors concluded that a vegetarian diet meets the nutritional requirements of all age groups, and that vegan diets comprising unrefined cereal products, legumes, nuts, vegetables, and fruits produce no detectable deficiency signs...proximate analysis of the vegan diets is remarkably normal, and the average nutrient intakes meet recommended daily allowances... An adequate percentage of useful protein is consumed by the vegans, and also not unexpectedly, by the vegetarians.

Ellis found that his subjects were no different healthwise than the normal population. He further notes that the vegan diet represents a much more efficient use of food than the normal omnivore's diet. However, he does still recommend B_{12} supplementation for vegans.

The only study conducted with the vegetarian sub-speciality, 'fruitarianism', that I'm aware of, was done at the turn of the century (Jaffa 1901). The small (in numbers) family, mentioned earlier, was also smaller than average in height and weight. The author postulated that this latter finding was probably due to hereditary factors. The family was in good health.

There are several reports of Vitamin B_{12} deficiency as the cause of serious illness in the breast-fed babies of vegan mothers. The cases, thus far, can be numbered on one's fingers but several are difficult to explain. In none are the mothers' diets included (Jadhav, Lampkin, Higginbottom) and this is a serious deficiency on the authors' part. Several of the mothers manifested an inability to properly absorb B_{12} for undisclosed reasons. Usually the mothers had a low serum B_{12} level but occasionally the serum B_{12} levels were inexplicably in the normal range. These puzzling cases represent a tiny fraction of the total possible (considering all vegans and vegetarians). Further work will have to be done in this area. Ellis in his study of large numbers of vegans states: "Vegans who have been on the vegan diet since birth are normally healthy." Most of the small number of sick babies reported, became ill at about 10 months of age. Higginbottom, whose otherwise excellent paper had earlier been criticized for mixing up the terms vegan, vegetarian and strict vegetarian, reports an interesting case. Several letters subsequently appeared in response. Frader reports a child with combined iron and B_{12} deficiency: Fleiss writes:

> Certainly, human milk may be inadequate in composition in a severely malnourished or sick mother; however, no known infant formula equals it. All women, during pregnancy and lactation, no matter what their eating philosophy, should, of course, ingest sufficient nutrients for their infants and themselves. A nutritionally adequate, strict vegetarian diet, is, in fact, possible. Natural vitamin B_{12} is synthesized by micro-organisms and, accordingly, vegans may obtain vitamin B_{12} from soy sauce (3 ug/5ml), miso and tempeh, as well as certain seeds and nuts, or by colonic synthesis when adequate unheated seeds are eaten (Register, UD: personal communication). Human milk from a healthy, well-nourished mother is a biocompatible, complete food for an infant's first four to six months of life without supplementation.

Acknowledging the rarity of this as yet undefined condition and its still undetermined mechanism, it would certainly still be wise for any breast-feeding vegan moms who have a sick child on their hands to see their local doctor for advice.

Finally, we should take note of a peculiar condition termed 'tobacco amblyopia'. A handful of papers have commented on the fact that several vegans who took up heavy smoking encountered a rare form of eye trouble. Indeed, Smith's two patients who developed a severe cord disease (sub-acute combined degeneration of the spinal cord) were vegan smokers. Whether their illness was related to their veganism is debatable, but it does appear possible that the cyanides in tobacco smoke somehow bind the B_{12} in the blood stream and render it unavailable to the body, precipitating a self-induced B_{12} deficiency state. The subject also merits more study.

Summaries can be dangerous, for as Mark Twain said: "after we get our facts straight we then distort them as we please." Some readers will have skipped to these conclusions directly and we owe them something of substance; the following points then are absolute, incontrovertible facts, graven on solid gold tablets in the vegan Hall of Fame.

1) After careful review of all the literature, often quoted as demonstrating 'pure' vegetarians often suffer Vitamin B12 deficiency because of inadequate dietary intake, not one solitary case was found wherein a vegan, consuming an adequate, purely plant food diet suffered any ill health due to Vitamin B_{12} deficiency or any other deficiency. This finding contradicts the statements made in virtually every textbook of medicine and nutrition I've come across. These books' statements are then usually passed about amongst other writers of texts, like a hereditary disease but in this case are not confirmed by a review of the evidence.

2) "In general the health of vegans is good and differs little from that of omnivores." (Ellis, 1971)

3) "Vegans who have been on the vegan diet since birth are normally healthy." (Ellis, 1971)

4) Male vegans have significantly lower serum cholesterol levels than male omnivores. This, along with their lower average weight, may be protective for coronary heart disease.

5) "Megaloblastic anemia of pregnancy does not occur in vegans."

6) Vegans have lower blood urea levels than omnivores.

7) No valid cases of megaloblastic anemia have been reported in vegans.

8) Vegans have 'normal', if not better, physical fitness and physical abilities compared to omnivores.

9) There is suggestive evidence that vegans will have lower rates of bowel cancer when compared with omnivores (studies not yet reported).

10) There is no evidence, as yet, that vegans suffer less from major illness than omnivores, although we all know that this must be a fact.

11) Although vegans (and vegetarians) have lower than 'normal' serum B_{12} levels, they enjoy full healthy lives and their diets meet all their nutritional needs.

Many other tid-bits are tucked away in the papers reviewed but will be left for the enterprising reader to glean. As soon as this writer gets over his love for chocolate ice-cream, he sees no valid, nutritionally-based concerns, which can deter him from becoming a full-*fudged* vegan.

There is a lot of stimulating material in these papers. Do vegetarians and vegans develop such altered metabolisms that they require less B_{12} than normal? Perhaps in vegans B_{12} is not a vitamin, perhaps it's only required in meat-eaters. There are many such thoughts which spring to mind but since most professionals would frown upon such idle speculation, we'll consider our reputation, such as it may be, and cease and desist.

Psychological Studies on Vegetarianism

Is madness the prerequisite to becoming a vegetarian or merely the result? This question has often been posed by detractors of the diet who feel, to paraphrase Mark Twain: "First God created fools, that was for practice. Then He created vegetarians." Well, any psychologist worth his Gestalt would certainly demand more accurate information. So, in this chapter we will clear up any misconceptions regarding the psychology or mental states of vegetarians by reviewing the pertinent literature—all four papers.

The popular view of mental illness (neurosis, psychosis, etc.), fostered in film and print, is of a group of gentle, sweet people, maligned by the world, who somehow—usually comically—manage to use their illness to illustrate assorted deep truths about the Mystery of Life. Yes, I enjoyed the allegory of the 'King of Hearts', too, but actual clinical experience with severe mental illness reveals, for the most part, people suffering great unhappiness and enduring severely fragmented lives. The creative, integrative aspects of psychosis have as yet to become apparent to this writer. If the literature shows vegetarians to be mental cases, then it is perhaps of no use even going on with this book (sigh). But luckily for us, most papers provide a view of our (vegetarians') mental states that is highly commendable and the one study that differs is so difficult to understand for those not familiar with the terminology that we'll possibly have to wait for clarification from the author.

Well, a vegetarian is not susceptible to mental illness.

There are a number of papers cited in other parts of this book which mention that in the vegetarians being studied for other reasons, no mental aberrations have been noted (such as eating meat?). McKenzie's 'Profile on Vegans' carries an appendix containing seven case histories detailing the reasons behind these persons' 'conversion' to veganism. A short sample:

> '...I was struck by how barbaric this was, and
> from there went on to realize that it was just as
> barbaric to kill animals and birds in order to eat

their flesh. I cannot say this was the starting point, but this is the first memory I have of even thinking about vegetarianism. I did not at this time know any vegetarians, and I was not sure it was possible to live without meat—also my family were against me, and I carried on with an orthodox diet for some time, though all the time knowing at the back of my mind that some day I would become a vegetarian...', which she soon did.

Most of the other cases express similar sentiments, being uniformly disturbed by the killing of animals for food and the incongruence of this action with the higher aspirations of mankind.

West compares the psychological health of vegans with two other groups, psychiatric out-patients (neurotics) and the Christadelphians, a minority religious group with no dietary restrictions. This study, published in 1972, used the 'Cornell Medical Index' (C.M.I.) to gauge the subjects mental abnormalities and concluded that:

> ...the vegans and Christadelphians are not shown to be neurotic or somatically ill by the C.M.I. whereas the neurotic patients show much higher scores than either minority group on both somatic and psychological sections. The obvious explanation is that vegans and Christadelphians are in fact no different from the normal population in health.

Additionally he remarked on Smith's study (1955) which,

> ...studied the relationship between food aversions and manifest anxiety in 425 students...and found high-anxiety individuals had a greater number of food aversions. The most disliked foods were brains, kidneys, liver, cottage cheese, and buttermilk. Vegetables and fruits were not often disliked. These aversions correspond closely to vegan avoidances, although the basis of choice is precisely formulated by the vegans on ethical grounds, but the comparison is not valid in the absence of findings of high anxiety in the vegans.

"It is a remarkable fact that the phenomenon of vegetarianism has never been the subject of a psychoanalytic paper" Friedman begins in 1974. "Equally interesting is the ease with which this condition can conjure up an etiological image—

namely, that vegetarianism must be related to depression and serve as a defense against oral cannibalistic wishes." (In response to Friedman, the author of *this* book finds another image conjured up, that of masses of vegetarian readers gnashing their teeth in despair.) But take heart, for this is only a review of one paper and...well, let's continue. "...when we consider that three-quarters of a century of psychoanalytic science has yielded not a single paper on vegetarianism, a sample of even one case merits discussion in the hope that additional clinical reports will yield a fuller understanding of this interesting and not rare condition." Friedman's first case of this 'interesting and not rare condition' concerns a 40-year-old man with "intermittent, unconscious vegetarianism" who suffered from chronic depression, retarded ejaculation, occasional impotence, hostility towards women and other nasty conditions. Since this patient was not a true vegetarian we are justified in not considering him in detail. Friedman considered that perhaps his unconscious vegetarianism (intermittent) is an appeal to his mother to return the breast to him after having given it over to his younger brother.

The second case is one of "true vegetarianism"; the terminology in the paper is at times difficult to understand unless you are in the field professionally. Nonetheless, let me briefly describe the case of the 27-year-old male who had been a vegetarian since age 5. His principal childhood fantasy about vegetarianism is recalled:

> The animals of the world have achieved dominance over man and are preparing to eat all humans. The patient is spared this fate, however, because he had refused to eat animals...If he ate meat, his noble flesh would be reduced to that of an animal and he would be filled with uncontrolled destructive animal urges.

He had several other associations with meat-eating and the interested reader is invited to peruse this paper in detail for more information. In his summary, the author states:

> The lack of full understanding of the ultimate etiology of vegetarianism was discussed, especially because defenses against cannibalism can only be described as a necessary but insufficient precondition for this phenomenon. The prominence of

contradictory identifications and concrete and literally understood introjective mechanisms was noted as possibly reinforcing the prohibition against eating meat. Speculations were made relating vegetarianism to vivid oral primal-scene impressions, and to its possible expression within the oral triad.

It has been awhile since this author has studied psychology formally and so I confess that presently I couldn't tell an oral triad from a trio. Friedman notes several other papers which have mentioned vegetarianism as a peripheral issue (in psychoanalysis).

We would be remiss if we did not take note of the evidence that vegetarianism is a stimulant to cleverness, if nothing else. A number of years ago, certain villagers in the Vilcabamba Valley, high in the Ecuadorian-Andes, were studied by a number of medical people in connection with their reported longevity. Numerous papers resulted, detailing the possible factors that enabled these old-timers to live so long; one of the factors noted was their vegetarian and low calorie fare. Subsequently, it turned out that they were old, but not that old. These old-timers apparently rewarded the attention they were receiving by aging about 20 years between studies (which were done every two years). When the jig was up they peacefully went back to their normal rate of aging. This is pointed out simply to demonstrate that not only is the vegetarian not susceptible to mental illness, he or she will probably turn out to be even more clever than average. Those seeking more than cleverness—actual wisdom, perhaps—will have to turn to veganism for fulfillment.

Does the mind or mental makeup of a vegetarian differ from the norm? If so does this difference evolve secondary to the diet or is it perhaps a precondition for adopting the diet? "Little effort has been made to determine the relationship between types of food on the one hand and the mind-body complex on the other.... I wish to deal here with one aspect of this question—vegetarianism—and review its relevance from historical, biological and contemporary perspectives." Thus spake Majumder in an interesting paper published in 1972.

If vegetarianism is to rise completely above the alleged status of a fad or blind faith, it must satisfy three major criteria: (1) from the nutritional point of view, vegetable diets must be complete with the standard daily requirements of the human body; (2) they must alleviate, if not eliminate, the food crisis in certain parts of the world; and (3) they must make positive contributions to the enhancement of 'bioethics' among the members of the next generation with regard to wildlife, agriculture, and conservation of natural resources.

Majumder discusses the energy transfer from the sun to our eventual food;

It is obvious that the harvest of available energy would be more efficient if more omnivores could be herbivorous. Many such animals (e.g., raccoons) change their food habit seasonally under the pressure of food scarcity, but we, the rational omnivores, can experiment with our food and respond to similar pressures with choices that are supported by cultural feasibility and nutritional studies. Scientifically, then, this argument may form the basis for vegetarianism.

The author subsequently investigates the data on the adequacy, nutritionally, of vegetarian diets:

Although substantial evidence indicates that vegetarian diets can be balanced to meet human requirements, research in this area is very limited. The scientific communities of affluent nations have an obligation to initiate such research in view of the frightening statistics which indicate that two-thirds of all children in the world—the future citizens of our planet—suffer from malnutrition owing to protein deficiency, while meat and fish proteins are out of their economic reach.

Then, more to the point regarding the subject of our present chapter, Majumder states:

Even less is understood about the primary effects of different types of food on human personality and behavior, I am not talking about the secondary (social) effects, such as the apparent linearity of 'starch food—obesity—self-consciousness'. Some empirical observations by early vegetarians, such as 'calming of spirit', 'allaying animal passion' and 'acuteness of mind' associated with their diets, can and should be subjected to scientific scrutiny.

This paper is clearly written so that the general reader would understand and benefit from its complete perusal. I think this last paragraph is an especially interesting proposal, although probably it would be a bear to obtain data on this sort of thing.

5

DISEASE AND VEGETARIANS

Introducing the Subject

All of the pro-vegetarian literature through the 1800s is infused with the idea that vegetarians suffer less from the bodily insults that most of mankind appears heir to. The later scientific literature on this subject is divided. In the following chapters the reader will find data indicating a possibly lowered incidence of major disease (such as certain types of cancer and of coronary artery disease) in vegetarians. The questions asked are whether this disease is due to the diet or to other related factors such as decreased smoking and alcohol abuse or perhaps some combination of related factors. There is still not much data indicating that vegetarians, even those on well-balanced diets, are miraculously spared physical illness to any significant extent. We will begin this present chapter by reviewing a few papers which concern themselves with a variety of medical conditions which do not readily fit into other portions of the book.

The first 'disease' noted is the peculiar disturbance in the body's use of copper, occurring in Wilson's disease. One of the manifestations of the disease is a most distinctive ring of golden-brown (Kayser-Fleisher rings) around the pupil of the eye, which is found in no other condition. Interestingly, in a 42-year-old mental patient, Giorgio et al., found such a ring in the absence of the disease. The patient was a vegetarian of sorts who drank huge amounts of carrot juice and developed rings in his eyes. Although the rings bore a striking superficial resemblance to Kayser-Fleisher rings, "they could be differentiated from them on three counts." We won't go into the details but to a medical person this is a most interesting case. Thus, while heavy abuse of alcohol can produce rings *around* one's eyes, the "carrotaholic" may develop rings in the eyes.

Another vegetarian did unto himself as no one else would have done unto him. Jagenburg reports on a fairly healthy gent who gradually changed to an almost bread and water diet. He became severely ill due to protein-calorie malnutrition. When he finally came to his senses and returned to an 'ordinary vegetarian diet' his return to health was swift and complete.

The next gent, reported by Leitner, was not so fortunate. A 48-year-old scientist developed a fatal infatuation with retinol and carrot juice, consuming up to 1,500,000 ug of retinol daily (daily recommended intake is 750 ug). The patient died of liver failure after about six years. (Retinol is a Vitamin A alcohol. I suppose this is proof that it's not nice to fool with Mother Nature).

The average paranoid vegetarian who takes the time to read some of the actual papers reviewed here will have little difficulty discerning the biases often exhibited in the scientific literature. As noted elsewhere, none seems as blatant as that originating in papers by 'nutritionists'. However, let us mute our outrage momentarily and consider the following interchange concerning 'hard core' vegetarians. Dwyer and Mayer of the Department of Nutrition at Harvard sent the following request to the *Lancet*:

> Sir;—we are engaged in a study of the motivations leading increasing numbers of American adults to become vegetarians. So far we have identified a number of different groups which vary with respect not only to motivation, but also to type of diet adopted, adherence to it, and other characteristics of lifestyle. Our greatest interest is the hard-core vegetarians—i.e. those who are the most committed to totally vegan diets and most strict in their observance of them—since we believe potential health risks are highest amongst such persons.... We have been struck in the course of our interviews with this third group by how many of them tell us that they took up their

form of vegetarianism as a reaction to very extended periods of 'hard drugs' use. The diets they adopt are rather bizarre;...our experience has convinced us that physicians and nutritionists should be extremely cautious in attempting to modify the eating habits of this subgroup *unless* they are clearly likely to endanger health, since we are increasingly convinced that in this case the adopting of these diets represents a crutch which helps them to refrain from relapsing into drug use...We would be most interested in hearing from any British colleagues who have made similar observations.

As this letter might seem somewhat provocative even to hard core readers, it understandably was but a short time before Dr. Mann sharpened his quill and galloped in to joust with the dragon:

Sir;—the density of errors is high in the letter of Dr. Dwyer and Professor Mayer. A vegan is one who takes no animal substance as food. Those who take only milk and eggs are called lacto-ovo-vegetarians. Both types are found among the Seventh Day Adventists. Hindus are expected to be vegans. The acknowledged authority on vegetarianism is Prof. Mervyn Hardinge, now Dean of the School of Public Health, Loma Linda University, Loma Linda, California. Dr. Hardinge wrote his Ph.D. dissertation on the health status of vegetarians. He found true vegans rare, even among SDA, and to have significantly more ill-health, especially anemia. (*See* chapter on Hardinge for more accurate picture.) Thus vegans do not have superior health. This work was actually done in the Dept. of Nutrition at Harvard. Dr. Mayer reminds me of the old Creole saying, 'the last thing a fish would discover is water'. The perjorative term 'hard-core', used repeatedly by Dr. Dwyer and Prof. Mayer to describe vegetarians is inappropriate. Would the author refer to a 'hard-core' Catholic, or a 'hard-core' Frenchman? This term, by usage, is reserved for criminality, and vegetarianism is not that. To contend without data, that vegetarianism is a crutch for drug usage, is also unfair. Our experience indicates that the recourse of American youth to vegetarianism is based on two rationalizations. Those who emphasize a doctrine of love do not wish to see animals victimized for food usage. The mistrust of the rambunctious food technologists who add chemicals with little attention to human safety leads many health conscious people to seek unprocessed, natural foods for their health protection. Thus many feel a vegetarian diet is the best recourse in an era of promiscuous manipulation of the food supply. Dr. Dwyer and Prof. Mayer, finally solicited only *confirmation* of their views. I suppose they intended to encourage *all* the facts and opinions."

Once again we see that it is a difference of opinion that makes a horse race.

The next case is rather unusual in that it involves an infection of a lifelong vegetarian, who had never eaten out (India), with a type of tapeworm which is contacted by non-vegetarians in the pork meat that they ingest. The patient appears to have done well with treatment but the source of infection remained unexplained. (*Cysticercosis with Taeniasis in a Vegetarian*; Prakash & Kumar, 1965)

We'll close this chapter with an interesting paper which raises several provocative points. In 1972, Ellis published a paper entitled 'Incidence of osteoporosis in vegetarians and omnivores'. Osteoporosis is a common and troublesome problem which may be thought of as being due to a decrease in the total quantity of bone in the skeleton. The bone that is present seems normal in its composition. Striking at any age, more commonly in oldsters, 'thinning of the bones' causes a good deal of pain and suffering all around. Low bone density is one of the criteria used to determine if the condition is present.

> The vegetarians included in this study had bone densities significantly greater than those of individually matched omnivores.... The results also suggest that vegetarians are less prone to osteoporosis than omnivores.... Bone density of the omnivores decreased with age; this was also seen in the vegetarian group but to a lesser degree. No further decrease in bone density appeared to take place in the vegetarians who were approximately 69 years old, whereas it continued to decrease in the omnivore group. These results suggest that there is less likelihood of vegetarians developing osteoporosis in old age.

The serum calcium in vegetarians was significantly lower than it was in the controls, however both levels remained within what we consider a normal range. Serum phosphate was normal in the vegetarians. Serum B12 levels were lower in vegetarians but this is almost always the case as the reader will have already discovered in perusing the previous chapters. Interestingly, folate levels were often lower than normal in the omnivores and finally the serum urea level (helpful in assessing kidney function) was significantly lower in the vegetarians. High levels tend to indicate a problem. The lower levels may be due to lower dietary intake of protein although vegetarian often have an absolutely average intake of protein and there may be other reasons for the finding.

There are undoubtedly many reports of diseases in vegetarians, but the vast majority concern those who are on deficient diets and thus will not be considered here.

The following two sections, dealing with vegetarianism and its relation to heart disease and cancer, respectively, provide some interesting information, especially for the non-adherent.

Human and environmental factors affecting disease are now coming under close scrutiny. Many different factors appear to contribute to the major health problems in Western society. I feel certain that one day the vegetarian way of life will be scientifically proven to be a positive force for good health.

Heart Disease and Vegetarians

Somewhere along the wild and wonderful coast of Nova Scotia lies a small community which is noted for the longevity of its inhabitants. One of the indigenous population, an ancient man, when interviewed by the CBC, was asked, "What is the death rate in this unusual community?" The grey-haired one pondered a few moments and then replied in his creaky voice, "Oh, about one per person." Well, even at one per person, the death rate from heart disease seems amazing. This is the number one killer, in the industrialized nations, of the adult population. It is related directly or indirectly to atherosclerosis. The latter term may be thought of as a condition caused by the deposition of lipids in the lining of the body's blood vessels, resulting in 'clogged pipes' (hardening of the arteries), with attendant heart attacks, strokes, and other nasty results.

In this chapter we'll deal with studies concerning themselves with heart disease (coronary heart disease—CHD), blood pressure, and related factors in vegetarians only. Some of the major risk factors known to be associated with CHD are increasing age, sex, diabetes, cigarette smoking, high blood pressure, and serum cholesterol levels. In the papers to be reviewed the reader will find one or another of these risk factors the subject of interest. A brief review of Chapter 1, section on General Nutrition may help the lay reader at this point, especially the segment on fats. Surprisingly, there are no clear-cut answers and, in spite of great volumes of studies, the scientists involved remain divided as to the real or fundamental cause (if any) for coronary heart disease. During the years that many of the following studies were conducted it was thought that fat and cholesterol in the diet resulted in high blood cholesterol levels and these high levels were, in turn, the factors causing atherosclerosis, leading to CHD. Investigation has revealed that populations with low cholesterol levels and low saturated fat intakes almost always have low rates of CHD. In the USA, persons with serum cholesterol levels above 260 mg per 100 cc, run an approximately four times greater risk of CHD than those persons with lower levels. It has been shown that cholesterol levels are raised by diets containing high levels of saturated fatty acids. Regarding vegetarians, we'll wait for the verdict revealed in the main portion of this chapter. Interestingly, children in the U.S.A. have much higher levels of cholesterol than are found in children in countries where the process of atherosclerosis is much less marked in adults.

The second Great War that engulfed the world, resulted in the 'material' that provided the subject matter of Steiner's paper 'Necropsies on Okinawans'. He states:

> ...the most striking finding was the low incidence of retrogressive and degenerative changes. Senility came late, and cardiac and skeletal muscles remained well preserved even in the aged. Arteriosclerosis also developed late and to a moderate degree or not at all, and its lethal sequels in the brain, kidneys and the heart were never seen.... After the life of these people had been studied, two possible etiologic factors appeared outstanding in explanation of the observations. They were:

1. a low tension, placid, although physically strenous life, and
2. a simple, predominantly vegetarian diet.

Related results, published in various papers, are discussed in Strom's study—"Mortality from circulatory diseases in Norway, 1940-1945." He marshals evidence indicating that:

...before the late war mortality from diseases of the circulatory system was rising each year in Norway. This rise ceased during the war and from 1941 to 1943-45 there was a well-marked fall in mortality from these diseases. Since the war there has been a rapid rise in mortality towards the pre-war level. The war-time decline in mortality was equally evident for both sexes and all ages; and it involved all the most important causes of death from circulatory diseases. This also applies to the post-war rise. The war-time decline coincided with severe dietary restrictions. The supply of calories was reduced, and this reduction was principally of foods containing fat, including those rich in cholesterol.

Thus the decrease in disease of the circulatory system, and the decline in mortality, essentially paralleled a decline in the use of foods obtained from animals, concomitant with a decline in the total caloric intake. Malmros agrees. "All this indicates that under normal conditions most Western peoples eat too much and that they would certainly get on well with a somewhat reduced supply of calories." He also noted the remarkably reduced mortality rates from arteriosclerosis in Finland, Norway, and Sweden during the 'lean' years of the war, along with the decline in the diabetic morbidity and mortality in connection with the reduced supply of foodstuffs:

There is much which goes to show that in Denmark, Sweden and the U.S.A. the consumption of eggs, butter, milk and other animalic fats is at present too high and may involve serious risks for public health.

It's fair to state that the evidence provided in these papers is only suggestive but certainly not conclusive.

Mirone authored two papers, the first in 1950 and the second in 1954, both dealing with her study of a vegetarian community (possibly religious, although the pertinent information is not provided). The subjects had been on the diet for periods ranging from 12-47 years. The diet did include milk and rarely, dried eggs (in cake). The men led very active lives in pursuing their occupations:

> Despite the fact that the subjects had been on a diet devoid of meat and low in animal protein for at least 12 years and in one case for 47 years, the blood findings fall within the normal range."

The blood tests obtained were sugar levels, iron, proteins, and studies of red and white cells. Her second paper added data on additional tests: uric acid, cholesterol, BUN and creatinine.

> Prolonged consumption of a diet low in animal protein (10-30 grams daily) had no apparent deleterious effect on the health of members of a community which did not eat meat...The serum cholesterol...levels were maintained at normal levels...

The cholesterol levels noted were all below 235 mg per 100cc. The vegetarian will read with mixed feelings her concluding statement:

> It appears that although meat adds zest and variety to meals, an adequate diet can be planned in its absence. Prolonged consumption of a vegetable diet which included skim milk was compatible with apparent good health.

In contrast, significantly lower cholesterol levels were revealed by the research conducted by Gupta and Pollak (among others) in vegetarians when compared with eaters-of-meat. Wynder's study of Seventh Day Adventists (SDA) disclosed the fact that in these predominantly vegetarian church members, men had a much lower rate of CHD than average, while the women were unchanged from the norm. The author relates this finding mainly to the much lower incidence of smoking in the SDA males when compared with the general population.

In the fifties and sixties a number of studies were published with the results of investigations conducted with Trappist monks (lacto-ovo-vegetarians) and Benedictine monks (average Western-style diet) as subjects. To make a long story short, the Trappists were found to have lower cholesterol levels than Benedictines and lower dietary intakes of fat (26% vs 46%) but nonetheless had roughly the same problems as their co-religionists with heart disease and complications of vascular disease. (Barrow, Calatayud, Patil, McCullagh, Groen, and others).

When pure vegetarian monks were studied, the results were definitely 'abnormal'. Lee studied Korean monks and nuns whose dietary fat intake averaged only 7%, none of this was obtained from animal sources. The serum cholesterol levels averaged 119 mg. per 100 cc. in the monks, while the nuns' levels were somewhat higher. These sedentary folk thus had remarkably low cholesterol levels, residing in the same ball park as Pygmies from the 'Congo'. The authors found it difficult to compare the amount of CHD with the other groups; however, "by history and electrocardiogram, the Buddhists would appear to have a very low incidence...of CHD and related diseases.

In 1963, a long study published in *Acta Medica Scand.* (this paper contains a very extensive bibliography), began:

> In the study of the etiology and pathogenesis of atherosclerotic heart disease much attention has been focused on the lipids of the serum. Many studies in animals and man indicate a relationship between the amount and kind of fat in the diet, concentration of lipids in serum, and occurrence of atherosclerotic disease...

The authors found a significantly lower level of blood lipids in the vegetarians and concluded that:

> ...it appears that the most important factors probably are the relatively low intake of fats here designated as a 'saturated type' and the relatively high intake of an 'unsaturated type'.... If for prophylactic (protective) reasons, a lowering of the serum lipids in the general population to the levels in the present vegetarian material (material?) is wanted...the necessary changes would probably be: a substitution of one-fourth to one-third of the 'saturated types' and a slight reduction of total fat intake.

These authors also point out that contrary to the findings in the normal population, vegetarian women do not increase their cholesterol levels markedly as they enter the menopause.

There are too many papers to conveniently review in a book of less than encyclopedic size, so we'll skip along, making certain that we touch on all the important points demonstrating the benefits of the marvelous vegetarian lifestyle.

Trowell (1972) states in his paper:

> Dietary fibre is derived from the cell wall of starch-containing plants. The fibre content of the food determines the transit time through the gastrointestinal tract and influences the weight, consistency, and bacterial content of the faeces. Those Western communities which take little fibre in their diet have a high incidence of coronary heart disease, especially if there are also other factors conducive to this disease, such as high consumption of fats, especially animal fats. These communities also have a high incidence of diverticular disease of the colon probably due to a low intake of fibre in the food.

Finally, Sacks, in a paper in the *New England Journal of Medicine*, revealed that the vegetarian subjects in his study of 'Plasma lipids and lipoproteins in vegetarians and controls,' had much lower cholesterol levels than non-vegetarians, lower triglyceride levels and somewhat lower values for various sub-groupings of serum lipoproteins. He found that consumption of dairy foods and eggs was associated with these findings but that body weight was not.

There exist certain abnormalities of serum lipoproteins with which doctors are familiar (various hyperlipoproteinemias), which respond, often reluctantly, to treatment. A 'rice' diet (Kempner) has been shown to be effective for some types and Sacks concludes:

> ...the vegetarian regimen offers a wider range of flavors and textures, and offers also the possibility that with further study...it might become an acceptable alternative treatment for some of these disorders.

Sacks' paper on blood pressure in vegetarians (Bostonians), and several other papers from various countries, reveals a strong association between low blood pressure and vegetarian diet and conversely, a higher blood pressure and an increased intake of animal foods. A typical pressure in a vegetarian would be approximately 110/70. The medical profession at present feels that any pressure greater than 140/80 in a young adult is abnormally high. Low pressures are now in vogue because they are associated with low rates of heart, kidney and blood vessel disease, low rates of stroke and appear to be associated with longevity. Lowenstein arrived at the same conclusion in his paper. Unfortunately for our vegetarian pride, 100% meat diets, such as in the Eskimos of Greenland, have also been associated with lower than average blood pressures.

What can we say in summarizing this somewhat confusing state of affairs? It is popularly thought that high cholesterol levels cause heart disease and that lowering these levels would prevent heart attacks. Most scientists would agree that this is still very much a hypothesis and that the problem is so complex that this simple answer will not suffice.

1. There is some evidence that vegetarians suffer less from all manner of circulatory system disease, including CHD, than non-vegetarians. The responsible factors have as yet not been isolated.

2. Vegetarians tend to have lower blood pressures than the average population, this being an advantage.

3. The increased intake of polyunsaturated fatty acids by vegetarians may be one of the main factors influencing No. 1 above.

4. Dietary intakes of fat in the normal population, average about 45%. A strict vegetarian, with an intake of about 7% has much lower level of cholesterol in the blood. This is, of course, also influenced by the low intake of animal fats which tend to contain more saturated fatty acids than plant fats.

5. In an effort to implicate sugar consumption as an important factor in the etiology of coronary heart disease, Walker found that although the evidence is incomplete, what is available does not significantly incriminate sugar. Ludkin presents opposing views and his paper so states:

   > "Vegans—among these people low intakes of sugar and refined cereals are usual.... Unfortunately, no attempt has been made, even by the relevant protagonists, to investigate this key type of population; there is only the impression that vegans have a relatively low prevalence of CHD."

6. Vegetarians are healthier, happier, and in superb physical condition, seldom dying (and then only at the bare minimum rate of one death per person). The vibrant good health of vegetarians is also a plus (except when you've been working all night and, despite great fatigue, are still so vibrant that you can't fall asleep).

Cancer and Vegetarianism

Cancer! This word packs tremendous emotional power in our society, most people equating this diagnosis with a death sentence. Yet, the term as commonly used represents hundreds of different types of malignancies, some of them very curable, others becoming increasingly treatable as time reveals new methods of treatment. The causes of some types of cancer are known (chemicals, radiation), certain types are familial. Certain types of cancer are associated with living in certain countries. For an even larger number of malignancies, scientists have their suspicions and are aware of a number of factors, which, if present, are almost invariably associated with the development of cancer. Diet is one 'variable' which is being studied to see if certain types of diet can either increase or decrease the incidence of various cancers. Whether one fundamental cause of cancer will ever be discovered appears doubtful.

A few papers dealing with vegetarians in this regard will be reviewed here, the Seventh Day Adventists (SDA) providing the experimental subjects. Other papers, not reviewed here do provide incidental evidence, i.e., "Necropsies on Okinawans" showed the low incidence of cancers in all but the older population. In 1959 Wynder et al., studied the incidence of cancers in a SDA population, whom we can consider to be non-smokers, non-drinkers, and largely vegetarian. In studying the SDA subjects, Wynder notes:

> ...marked differences were found in the incidence of cancer of the lung, mouth, larynx and esophagus. The observed values were 8 times less than the expected values. The sex ratio of these cancers among Seventh Day Adventists was unity (i.e., men and women were equally as susceptible to these cancers). This holds true even

for that population group living in a city such as Los Angeles, which has a special air pollution problem. Among men, cancer of the bladder, and among women, cancer of the cervix, occurs to a statistically significant degree with less frequency among Seventh Day Adventists than among other religious groups.

Several other types of primary cancer were found decreased in SDA subjects, but not significantly so when studied statistically. It is not possible to state exactly what proportion of these findings might be due to diet and what proportion is secondary to non-smoking and other good habits.

A subsequent preliminary paper in 1964 by Lemon, again dealing with SDA subjects, came to somewhat similar conclusions. It showed that smoking cigarettes was strongly associated with certain types of cancer of the respiratory system. All cancers in general were down, yet not significantly when statistical indices were used. Lemon's conclusions were published in 1966.

> The total number of deaths observed and death from respiratory disease were approximately one half and one fourth, respectively, of that expected at comparable ages for California men.... The findings from this study are consistent with previous epidemiologic studies and predictions of a large reduction in lung cancer and other mortality in any non-smoking U.S. population. The findings support the causal relationship of cigarette smoking to lung cancer...

There's not much to say about diet in this regard except it would probably be better to eat the tobacco than to smoke it.

Although we haven't seen much direct evidence for dietary influence on cancer thus far, there is much evidence, not always dealing specifically with vegetarians, which appears to indicate that meat ingestion *is* associated with certain types of cancer. For example, Cunningham, in 1976, published a paper in the *Lancet* which indicated the following:

> Human lymphomas (a type of cancer) may result from a combination of genetic and environmental factors. Nutrition has hardly received any attention as a possible factor, though two observations suggest that over-nutrition, especially of protein

may be a factor in the pathogenesis of lympho-mas...(Pathogenesis means—to generate a dis-eased condition).

Geographic comparison reveals a positive cor-relation between consumption of animal protein, particularly bovine (beef) protein, and lymphoma mortality. Allied observations suggest that ex-cessive consumption of animal protein may, through antigen absorption and chronic persis-tent stimulation, impose considerable wear and tear on lymphoid tissue and thereby encourage malignant changes.

The reader will note a good deal of 'may' and 'suggest' in this literature as the evidence is at present only suggestive. In the next few years however, we can expect researchers to come up with a more definite 'maybe' regarding some of these questions.

There is research currently being conducted which should prove to be very interesting. In this context we refer to a letter by Ellis in the *British Medical Journal*:

...we agree it would be of interest to know if the incidence of cancer of the large bowel is apprecia-bly lower in vegetarians than in the rest of the population. At present it is estimated that there are between 100,000 and 500,000 vegetarians in Britain. For some years we have been studying the incidence of disease in vegetarians. The find-ings so far would indicate that there is no appar-ent difference in the incidence of cancer in general between vegetarians and the rest of the popula-tion...we are currently investigating the incid-ence of all cancers and other diseases of the ali-mentary tract in vegetarians and hope that this may throw some light on the matter.

The scientific investigation of the relationship between diet and cancer has just begun. There are scientific suspicions that certain types of cancer are related to eating meat but, at present, no definite proof exists. A large variety of known cancer-causing substances have been found in meats with still others formed after cooking, but still one can't say that they actually cause cancer in the human. We're being cautious here; but if one were a meat-eater, it would be difficult not to be uneasy about certain suspicions. Fortunately, there are no indications that vegetarian diet is associated with anything but epidemic good health.

Macrobiotics

Ancient Chinese philosophy envisioned the universe as in constant flux, waxing and waning, symbolized by the concepts of Yin and Yang. The interdependence of humanity and nature was seen in the interplay between these 'forces'. Thus, nutritionally, one would select a diet that maintained a state of harmony (certain foods being more Yin than Yang and vice versa).

In the past few decades, the Zen dietary 'system' of George Oshawa (b. 1893), based on these concepts, has become quite popular. This fellow, who supposedly cured himself of an incurable disease by living solely on a brown rice diet, devised a system of diets, numbered from -3 (allowing nearly all foods) to +7 (exclusively brown rice). As one progressed along from the lower to the higher forms, good health resulted, diseases were cured and harmony with the universe was restored. The nutritional basis in diet #+7 stemmed from "transmutation" of the rice into all necessary food factors. Most aspects of eating are regulated in this system; chewing, fluid intake, etc. Macrobiotics is included under the "disease" heading only because the papers dealing with Macrobiotics usually report cases of malnutrition of one sort or another. As numerous healthy macrobiotic practitioners, usually adhering to the lower diets, exist, we must acknowledge that the view presented by the scientific literature is misleading.

When I first came across George Oshawa's writings on Macrobiotics, especially living on brown rice alone, I thought, "You can't be Ceres!." Now, although I did not believe his claims that the diet would cure *all* illness it did seem worthy of experimental verification for two reasons, its promise to halt the premature demise of a fine head of hair, and its promise of spiritual enlightenment. My dear friend and future wife aided me in this quest and within two weeks we were rapidly enlightened of 30 lbs. total. We chewed all our food 30 times, watched our water intake, and lived on boiled rice. One day, as my dear friend crawled over to visit me, brushing past the ghost of Dr. Stark, we realized that we must eat something else. Baldness would have to wait another cure. We did compromise for several days by sniffing the mustard jar, in addition to eating the brown rice, but even this left a longing for more in our hearts.

Well, in rapid progression we dropped all the way down through the diets until we ended up at the malt shop sipping chocolate milk shakes.

Many vegetarians fare much better on the diet than we did, usually utilizing one of the lower diets. The literature on Macrobiotics is concerned mainly with nutritional disease which has occurred in people living on the highest diets exclusively. I understand that some revision of Oshawa's system is occurring, that renders obsolete the dangers of the higher diets. It should be noted also that the lower diets are not necessarily vegetarian as flesh foods are allowed. The literature on Macrobiotics is not voluminous and the reader should be forewarned by the paragraph above about my unfounded prejudices regarding the diet.

The first paper we'll consider deals with a lady who lived on the # + 7 diet for six months and nearly died of scurvy. Sherlock details her illness and her recovery in some detail. He notes that the diet is a danger for two reasons; one, the most rigid (# + 7) diet is nutritionally inadequate and, two, the philosophy encourages people to cure their illnesses with the diet, with the resultant delay of therapy should serious illness befall the practitioner.

In 1966, the Passaic Grand Jury was presented with documented evidence, by medical workers and others, of a number of deaths in young people due solely to adherence to the higher Macrobiotic diets. The jury urged people to use extreme caution in considering or using the diet.

The Council of Foods and Nutrition (AMA), in 1971 discussed the 'problem' of Zen Macrobiotic Diets. Again, the feelings expressed were identical with those of Sherlock:

> Individuals who persist in following the more rigid diets of Zen Macrobiotics stand in great danger of incurring serious nutritional deficiencies, particularly as they progress to the highest level of dieting.

A subsequent letter, by Rosebury, traced the problem of 'fad' diets to the general "anti-science" attitude prevalent these days.

Robson et al., studied two infants fed "Kokoh", a macrobiotic food preparation consisting of cereal grains, legumes, and oil seeds. Part of the problem with the underweight infants lay with the adulteration of their formula with water. The authors felt that the composition of the formula was probably adequate for growth in children, but that it needed to be fed in higher concentrations, whereas, in these cases, it was actually being diluted, with resulting malnutrition.

Several jargon-filled papers by Erhard make note of a small number of children who suffered various sorts of deficiency diseases due to being fed inadequate diets by their Macrobiotic parents. Despite the jargonistic features of Erhard's papers, very important information is developed. She reveals the existence of a 'voluntary' form of malnutrition in a very small number of children of Macrobiotic parents. While earlier cursing the use of terms such as 'faddists' and 'cultists' in reference to vegetarianism as a whole, it does appear that a tiny minority of "vegetarians" 'live' on very inadequate and abnormal diets because of certain beliefs. Children fed these inadequate diets do very poorly. Again, we are not dealing here with the usual, normal vegetarian or vegan population.

Reports come from Britain which are very similar in nature to the above report (*British Medical Journal*, vol. 1, 1979, p. 296). These authors suggest prosecution of the parents for 'child abuse'. The parents in this handful of cases appear 'deaf to reason' and while the malnourished children did well when hospitalized and fed normally (vegetarian), there was great resistance from the parents to treating these obviously sick youngsters.

Despite fanciful speculation upon the future of nutrition elsewhere in this book, there are limits to dietary changes, which, once transgressed, result in damage to the well-being of the persons involved. Well-rounded vegetarian and vegan diets have fueled the growth and development of uncounted lives. Hopefully, these reports of 'voluntary' malnutrition are not indicative of a larger, as yet undetected, problem.

Brown and Bergan (1975) express several concerns regarding the Macrobiotic diet, uncovered by their study of eight Macrobiotic subjects (which included one infant). They found that according to the recommended nutrient levels, the diets, especially the higher ones, were lacking in calories, calcium, and riboflavin. Low or marginal protein intakes were worrisome:

> These problems can be alleviated in the adult by increased consumption of foods within the

Macrobiotic dietary regimen; in the infant, by the inclusion of milk, although iron would still be a potential problem. The limitations of this diet become emphasized when it is applied to the growing child and they may be severe enough to result in depressed physical development.

Finally, Brown and Bergan published the results of a study of fifty adults and ten children who 'followed' the macrobiotic diet. The adults averaged twenty-eight years of age and were all in good health and "...the base of their diet was grains interspersed with a wide variety of vegetables, fish, cheese, and eggs...". Perceived difficulties with the limitations in energy, calcium, and riboflavin intake could be remedied by increasing the amounts eaten. The women were deficient in iron. These values were, of course, calculated and compared to the RDA (recommended daily allowance).

The final line of these papers thus appears to be a damnation of the highest numbered (up to #+7) Macrobiotic diets, on a nutritional basis, along with the recommendation that infants have their diets supplemented with milk, and that adults make certain that they obtain sufficient quantities of the foods they select. Other than the fatalities due to the higher diets, the diet appears to sustain life. I don't know if the metaphysical promises are fulfilled for others, but my personal experiment illustrated that I had not then gotten the hang of Yang. Macrobiotic practitioners, however, assure us—the "normal" vegetarians—of the great benefits bestowed by this approach to life.

Zealots, Faddists, and Nutritionists

It is unfortunate, but true, that there is in existence a genre of scientific literature equivalent to the 'pulp magazine'. Although these journals have published numerous excellent papers on vegetarianism, (Hardinge's paper for example), in general, one often finds their quality of papers to be poor and the articles often to be unscientific and filled with demeaning jargon. The authors, usually 'nutritionists', freely employ such demeaning terms as 'cultists', 'zealots', 'hard-core vegetarians', etc., when referring to this sublime way of life. It can be unpleasant literature to wade through and appears to present the worst of the scientific (so-called) literature available to the reader of vegetarianism.

As noted, the first two terms used in this chapter heading are used in these journals to denote those who follow unAmerican dietaries, such as vegetarian fare. These categorizations actually date back hundreds of years, only the people they are applied to are changing. Undoubtedly there are faddists and zealots in every field of endeavor, spreading their particular brand of salvation, but this certainly doesn't apply to us vegetarians.

Hill, in 'Foods and Fads', systematically debunks everything that we hold sacred nutritionally, as vegetarians, but is forgiven for he does provide a good story of 'health-foodism' run amok.

> The final favorite is crude black molasses.... Nearly 200 years ago John Wesley in his 'Journal' recorded that after a cold wet journey on horseback he used to rub himself all over with hot black treacle (black molasses) before going to bed in order to ward off a cold. It is not very surprising to read later in the 'Journal' that his wife left him, Wesley's comment on this unfortunate event being, 'I did not ask her to go; I shall not ask her to return'. Black treacle as Wesley used it evidently failed to enhance his attractions...

American Institute of Nutrition—Food Faddism and Public Health (Sebrell):

> Vegetarian diets should probably be placed in this category—fads derived from fear of foods. Behind the early writings on the subject, one can usually discern the idea that meat arouses animal passions and is therefore inimical to philosophic and spiritual thought. Nutritionists do not challenge the statement that humans can subsist on a non-meat diet...Among vegetarian races, signs of protein deficiency are frequent, whereas a heavy meat diet is quite compatible with good health and development.

Written on a somewhat higher level is the paper by Todhunter entitled 'Food habits, Food Faddism and Nutrition' (1973) where vegetarianism is found under the heading of 'Cults':

Hippocrates wrote of the health value of certain foods, and fads of various kinds have persisted ever since. One can understand the existence of myths and fallacies about food in earlier times; but why does it exist today when over the past 100 years scientific knowledge about nutrition and foods has developed to a high degree and with current research continuously adding new knowledge? Olson believes faddism persists because food has emotional rather than intellectual value to the average person;.... Fads provide a means of satisfying the emotional needs...Vegetarianism is not necessarily quackery unless it professes to cure illness...Many vegetarians believe that the kind of food one eats is of the utmost importance in leading a contented and harmonious life and that it encourages development of the intellect, increases the capacity for mental labor and promotes longevity...Interest in the vegetarian movement has waxed and waned over the last 2 centuries and has now revived...The 'hippies' of the younger generation have used diet as a revolt against the 'Establishment'....

In the early '70s a variety of nutritionists discovered these 'New Vegetarians' and rushed into print with a generally forgettable series of papers related to their beliefs and habits. These papers, while presenting some useful information tend rather, to give bias a bad name. For example, after reading Erhard's papers I have to agree with a letter to the editor:

Sirs: I am very disappointed in Darla Erhard's article, 'The New Vegetarians.' I find this article anti-intellectual, supercilious, and offensive...

Another letter:

Sirs: In her article, Mrs. Erhard describes some of the horrors of the new vegetarian and life philosophy diets. Is it not possible for her to respect their culture while providing nutritional knowledge that could be incorporated into the lifestyle and philosophy of the people she is 'trying' to help? I feel that Mrs. Erhard, like many other nutritionists, finds herself totally polarized from her client population...

It is strange, that of all people, it is mainly those working in the field of nutrition who do not appear to realize the strong emotional connection people and food have, and that to criticize or demean a person's diet is often tantamount to criticizing the individual directly.

And last, from the *British Medical Journal*, 'Food Revisionists':

> Few research workers are prepared to be dogmatic about disciplines other than their own—except in nutrition, where any old scientist (and not a few lay people) feel sufficiently qualified to pronounce authoritatively on the essentials of a good diet...

The author then discusses the various aspects of macrobiotic and related diets, concluding:

> Doctors, nutritionists, dietitians, and public health workers should be aware of these diets and should be careful to try to re-educate, sympathetically, the adolescents who believe in them. Basically, most food-fad diets have much to recommend them and probably need only minor corrections, without any need for derogatory comment about the underlying assumptions. We ought to recognize and respect the emotional importance of food to these adolescents and the underlying religious connotations. Indeed their attitude to food in these days of incipient world shortages is perhaps preferable to the waste and excess which most of the rest of us so unethically demonstrate.

Nutritional science is a fascinating subject and reading in the associated literature is as interesting as reading a popular novel. Thus, the disappointment engendered by the poor quality of literature and the narrow-mindedness of many of the authors, is all the more difficult to bear.

> He felt like a man who, chasing rainbows, has had one of them suddenly turn and bite him in the leg.
>
> —P.G. Wodehouse

6

UPDATE

Fresh Food for Thought

Included in this section are brief reviews of a number of papers which were previously unavailable to me. Since I have come to London, where modern vegetarianism had its institutional roots, I am able to rectify this problem. First, I will review two papers which do for rational thought what the Titanic did for ocean cruising. These two *pseudo*-scientific classics were published in the Fall 1977 issue of *Pediatrics* and Spring 1978 issue of *J. Am. Diet. Assoc.* The authors studied a group of Bostonian 'vegetarian' children, measuring weight, height, skin fold thickness (one measure of the body's nutritional state), head circumferences and calculated the 'growth velocities' from the data. Just a few examples of errors, (of the many available), will be noted. The initial design of the study is poor. Due to the classification system, almost half of the 72 subjects could have been eating red meat daily, yet be included. These 'macrobiotic' diets are not adequately characterized.

The 'vegetarians' were compared with two groups, one of which was a group of contemporary omnivorous children. Both of these papers are about the same study, with the data just worked into the two papers in traditional fashion.

In one paper the authors state that:

> ...the vegetarian subjects' measurements were not only lower for weight, length and triceps than

might be accepted from standards but were also lower than the non-vegetarian children's measurements.

The other paper states that:

...the size at first measurement was less than the Harvard standards but differences between vegetarian children were not apparent.... Neither did they differ from non-vegetarian children measured at the same time.

And what did they say about subscapular skinfold measurements?

However, vegetarians did not differ from non-vegetarians in their subscapular measurements, although both groups exhibited measurements which were much below those expected...data were not analyzed further for this variable.

Thus, after having our confidence in the accuracy of their data totally shattered we turn our attention to the second group with which the 'vegetarians' are compared, variously referred to as the 'norm', 'Harvard norm', 'Harvard standard', and 'Harvard Longitudinal Study of Child Health and Development.' This 'normal' group of 134, mainly Irish Bostonian (presumably meat-eating) subjects, studied from 1930 to 1956, are quite dissimilar to the present 'vegetarians' in many ways, even to the basis of their selection.

Is this group a good group to compare the 'vegetarians' with, using the former as a 'norm' or 'standard'? Reed, one of the producers of the early study and also a co-author of the present study wrote in 1959:

Individual children differ widely between themselves in all attributes at any given age. The distribution of values for a given attribute at any given age has a characteristic form, but the means as well as the extremes of the ranges tend to differ considerably between groups.... The careful observation, assessment and recording of values or ratings for various aspects of growth and development of populations of children of specified ages adds to knowledge of the extent of individual influences, which in turn permits better understanding of the findings on individual cases within such populations.

He continues, and I would like to emphasize his next statement: "They do not however permit definition of the limits of normality." Finally, Reed notes:

> Such data have greater value when the children from whom they were derived have been studied from other points of view such as the incidence of illnesses, general health and nutrition. When those holding a unique or fringe position within the range for any one attribute can be studied in respect to these other factors, more light can be thrown upon the possible importance of such a position to them.

In 1978 the authors wrote:

> "...other differences, such as illness...were not investigated and cannot be excluded as alternate explanations."

Despite all the above, Dwyer, Reed and group leapt to many conclusions: "In the present study the growth velocities of vegetarian infants and pre-school children are variable and often differ from norms" (i.e., the Harvard standard noted above) "and therefore the adequacy of some of the children's diets is suspect". Actually, it's their whole paper that is suspect. But wait, there's more. "If, however, the growth retardation found among vegetarian pre-school children suggests a less than optimal nutritional or health status, it would have little to recommend it."

Growth retardation? I thought, becoming somewhat hysterical...but read on. "Vegetarian children's growth should be closely monitored. If intervention efforts to maintain growth velocities within norms are to be undertaken...." At this point I fainted and slid under the table—no, it's not funny. In plain English, the authors, presuming their data are somewhat accurate (and we've seen them discard that information which didn't fit a preconceived notion), would suggest that these *often meat-eating 'vegetarian' children* should follow the growth patterns obtained by a study of 134 Bostonian children of several decades ago and that we should intervene to ensure that they do! It might be possible as long as another group doesn't complain and attempt intervention to maintain growth velocities similar to those of a hundred Icelandic-American children from Skokie.

"Vegetarian children's growth should be closely monitored." For the first time in any paper that I've come across, the authors state that a few "children were so uncooperative that physical measurements could not be taken" and were thus dropped from the study. (Perhaps these were the large-sized vegetarians who are missing from the study.) In any case, it appears that it might be difficult to monitor their growth.

Can anything useful be taken from these papers? Even barring the authors unjustified and self-contradictory statements, I personally feel there is little of significant value here. (P .001)

The American Academy of Pediatrics Committee on Nutrition wrote a standard paper in 1977 on 'Vegetarianism' which, aside from the usual chit-chat ("Vitamin B_{12} deficiency occurs in pure vegetarian diets after a variable period because this vitamin is derived exclusively from animal products.'") is fairly innocuous.

Cases of Vitamin B_{12} deficiency in children on adequate vegetarian diets are probably non-existent but we've noted earlier several puzzling cases in infants, a few of whom had vegan mothers. Several papers have been published describing problems, fairly esoteric defects, in the absorption, transport, and handling of Vitamin B_{12} in some children. As more of these cases are studied, the problem of whether there is really a problem (from our limited point of view regarding the diet), should be eventually resolved.

Additional References

1. Johanna T. Dwyer et al. *J. Am. Dietet. A.* 72:264-70, 1978

2. Committee on Nutrition, *Pediatrics* 59:460-64, 1977

3. Margaret W. Shull, et al. *Pediatrics* 60:410-17, 1977

Like Getting Blood from a Turnip?

1. Serum cholesterol and triglyceride levels (fasting), in 22 vegans and 22 omnivores, were obtained. Briefly, the concentration of both "were significantly lower in the vegans than in the omnivores". Because of several factors related to the diet the authors suggest that: "a vegan diet may be the diet of the choice for the treatment of certain types of hyperlipidaemia."

This latter (hyperlipidaemia) is a group of abnormalities of lipids in the blood.

—Sanders and Ellis, *Proc. Nutr. Soc.*, 36(1) 43A May 1977.)

2.   A study of 28 vegan pregnancies and 41 control pregnancies (omnivores) revealed the following. The first pregnancy in vegans (none of whom took B_{12} supplements; 22% used iron supplements) occurred at 30 years compared to 25½ years in omnivores. No significant differences were noted between the two groups in pre- and post-natal health status, stillbirths, toxemia and anemia. Birth weights of babies were 'normal'.

> This study shows that vegan women undergo pregnancy whilst continuing their vegan diet without any adverse effect on themselves or their offspring, the only difference being the increased incidence of breast feeding which is a positive advantage to the child.
>
> —Thomas and Ellis, *Proc. Nutr. Soc.*,
> 36(1) 46A, May 1977.

3.   Several mammals appear to require a dietary source of long-chain polyunsaturated fatty acids (LCP FA) for "optimum health", not being able to manufacture them from shorter chains. Long-chain polyunsaturated fatty acids are:

> ...absent from higher plants...we have investigated man's ability to produce LCP FA from (short-chain polyunsaturated fatty acids, SCP FA) by studying vegans, whose diet contains no LCP FA, in comparison with omnivores.

The authors found:

> ...total polyunsaturated and SCP FA were considerably greater in the vegans than in the controls but the proportion of LCP FA was similar in both groups.... Clinical and biochemical examination of the subjects yielded no evidence of ill health in any of the subjects...there is no evidence that a source of LCP FA is necessary in the human diet.
>
> —Sanders and Ellis, *Pro. Nutr. Soc.*,
> 35(3) 125A-127A, Dec., 1976.

4.   Angina Pectoris, i.e., chest pains related to poor blood or oxygen supply to heart muscle, often precedes 'heart attacks'. Ellis put four patients with 'severe' angina on a vegan diet. They all improved dramatically over a period ranging from

weeks to months. Having followed these patients for up to 10 years Ellis states:

> ...there is a considerable body of evidence to suggest that a diet devoid of animal products may have certain advantages in the prevention and possible treatment of ischemic heart disease and angina pectoris. We believe these findings are sufficiently significant to warrant a controlled trial to evaluate whether a diet devoid of animal produce is effective in treating angina pectoris.
>
> —Ellis, F.R., *American Heart Journal*, 93 No. 6, June 1977.

5.   Another paper from the above author, along with Sanders and Dickerson, entitled "Haematologial Studies on Vegans", determined that these 34 vegans (6 of whom were "born to and breast fed by vegan mothers and weaned and reared on a vegan diet"), were all in good health and their diets (the majority took B12 supplements) promoted "good blood formation".

[Sanders & Ellis, *Br. J. Nutr.*, 40(9) 9-15 July 1978]

6.   Further blood work on vegans revealed amongst other things, that "weights, skinfold thickness, serum vitamin B_{12}, cholesterol, and triglyceride concentrations were less than those of controls. In conclusion, the authors felt that the "vegan type diet may be the one of choice in the treatment of ischemic heart disease, angina pectoris and certain hyperlipidemias." Results of this study (Sanders and Ellis, F.R., *Am. Journal of Clin. Nutr.*, 31:805-813, 1978) have shown up in other papers noted above.

7.   A number of letters (pro and con) to *Lancet* resulted from Rose's letter 25 September 1976 stating that Asian immigrants to Britain suffered often from B_{12} deficiency due to "vegan dietary habits adopted in Britain."

8.   —Hirwe, R., *J. Biosoc. Sci.*, 8, 221-227, 1976. Vitamin B_{12} and Potential Fertility in Male Lacto-vegetarians.

9.   Inamdar-Deshmukh, A.B., *Br. Journal of Haem.* 32:395-401, 1976. Healthy Indian lacto-vegetarians were compared with non-vegetarians. Routine blood tests (WBC, RBC, etc.) and mean erythrocyte Vitamin B_{12} levels showed no difference between the two groups while the serum B_{12} levels in vegetarians were lower than normal, as shown often in the past.

10. —Carmel, R. *Ann. of Int. Med.*, 88:647-649, 1978. Nutritional Vitamin B12 Deficiency: possible contributory role of subtle Vitamin B12 Malabsorption.

11. Jackson, W.P. et al., *S. Afr. Med. J.*, 53(22) 880-1, 3 June 1978. Studied a group of Indian lacto-vegetarians and found them to be somewhat overweight due to consumption of large amounts of food, with a tendency to higher blood sugars (11% were diabetic). "Certainly this sort of vegetarianism did not protect against overweight or hyperglycaemia".

12. Eddy & Taylor, with the assistance of the Research Section of the Vegetarian Society (UK), studied 22 elderly vegetarians (some were vegetarian since childhood), noting that their general knowledge of diet was better than average and that they maintained a "high vitamin-status" with regard to Vitamin C & B-group. A number of implications are discussed.
—Eddy, T.P., *Age Ageing*, 6(1) 6-13, Feb. 1977.

13. —Harland and Peterson, *J. Am. Diet. Ass.*, 72, 259, March 1978. "Nutritional Status of lacto-ovo-vegetarian Trappist Monks."

14. —Finegold, et al., *Am. J. Clin. Nutr.*, 30:1781-1792, Nov. 1977, "Fecal Microbial Flora in Seventh Day Adventists". This study deals with the question of 'diet-bowel-cancer-bacteria'. Adventists have lower rates of large bowel cancer, as we've noted before, but vegetarian Seventh Day Adventists don't seem to have lower rates than non-vegetarian Seventh Day Adventists. These authors also note that non-vegetarian Utah Mormons have even lower rates than vegetarian Seventh Day Adventists. Regarding this study, differences were found between bowel flora of different groups, but any practical significance remains to be seen.

Hopefully, the next few years will see the beginning of more studies on vegetarians, ones that are fairly scientific. A longitudinal growth study on Western vegetarian children, appropriately categorized would be welcomed.

Armstrong, *Am. J. Epid.*, 105(5) 444-9, May 1977.

Vymeister, "Safe Vegetarian Diets For Children". In *Ped. Clin. N. Am.*, 24(1) 203-210, Feb. 1977.

Whorton, *J. Hist. Med.*, 32(2) 115-139, April 1977.

7

SUMMARY

Considering the great importance of vegetarians—probably more than one-half of the world's population at present—the amount of English scientific literature extant actually reflects a relative lack of scientific interest in their feeding and care. Nonetheless, the data that have been discussed in this book, while still rather sketchy, should have laid to rest any fears one might have had that vegetarianism is an inadequate dietary resulting in poor health and other undesirable conditions. We've seen that vegetarians who ingest adequate diets are well-nourished from conception to old age. Vegans, who restrict their diets to plant food alone, also do well in every sphere of human endeavor.

Inadequate diets reveal their ill-effects in omnivores as well as in herbivores and a vegetarian doesn't seem anymore able to live on 'tea and buns' alone than does a meat-eater. Conversely, well-nourished vegetarians do very well in athletic competition, appear to have reduced rates of heart disease, and possibly lowered rates of various types of cancer, especially of the large bowel. These latter findings will be clarified with further research but the suggestions are there.

Vegetarians are the most efficient form of human life, based on energy transfer from sun to man. The World Health Assembly (1977) concluded that the potentially single greatest public health problem by the turn of the century would not be cancer or heart disease, but rather, malnutrition. The economics and superior nutrition of adequate vegetarian dietaries are thus even more compelling.

The evolution of the human mind, arising from the long course of evolution of physical forms, is leading us closer to the concepts of consciousness in non-human creatures. When humanity, as a whole, recognizes the nature of the sentient creature which it now slaughters for food, then we'll have reached the end of a long, unpleasant chapter in humanity's nutritional history.

The knowledge that we presently possess is reasonably suggestive of the idea that the most acceptable diet for humans is the one which is most economic, least pathogenic or, more positively, most 'healthogenic', and most ethically derived. Vegetarianism fits this description perfectly.

I hope the vegetarian reader has learned something about the scientific basis for this diet, and the non-vegetarian likewise. This writer will now excuse himself as it is time for his daily mile-run. (Be back in three minutes.) But, I leave you with these words—

Deliver us
Herbivorous!

BIBLIOGRAPHY

Acott, K.M. "Yogurt: Is it truly Adelle's B-vitamin factory." In *Food Prod. Devel.*, 6:50, 1972.

Abernathy, R.P. "Lack of response to Amino Acid Supplements by Pre-adolescent Girls". In *Amer. J. Clin. Nutr.*, 25:980, 1972.

Adler, S. "Suppressive effect of a meat diet on infections of Plasmodium vinckei in mice". In *Harefuah*, 54(3):63, 25 Feb., 1958.

Adolph, W.H. "Vegetarian China" In *Sci. Am.* 159·133 Sept. 1938

Alcott, W.A. *Vegetarian Diet: As sanctioned by medical men and by experience in all Ages.* N.Y.: Fowler and Wells, 1938.

Alsted, G. "Exogenous Pernicious Anemia". In *Am. J. Med. Sc.*, 197:741, 1939.

Alther, L. "Organic farming on trial". In *Natural History*, 81:16, 1972.

Altschul, A.M. "Proceedings: Potential for vegetable proteins in prudent diet foods". In *Prev. Med.*, 2(3):378, Nov., 1973.

———. "The revered legume". In *Nutr. Today*, 8:22, 1973.

Altschuler, S.S. "The history and biological evolution of human diet". In *Am. J. Dig. Dis.*, 1:215, 1934.

Anderson, M.A. "Nutritional knowledge of health food users in Oahu". In *Am. Diet. Assoc. J.*, 67(2):116, Aug., 1975.

Appledorf, H. "Health foods vs traditional foods". In *J. Milk Food Technol.*, 36:242, 1973.

Aries, V.C. "Effect of vegetable diet on fecal flora and fecal steroid concentration". In *J. Pathol.*, 103(1):54, Jan., 1971.

Armstrong, B.K. "Hematological, Vitamin B_{12} and folate studies on Seventh Day Adventist vegetarians". In *Am. J. Clin. Nutr.*, 27(7): 712, Jul., 1974.

Arora, R.B. "Sperm studies on Indian men". In *Fert. Steril.*, 12:365, July-Aug., 1961.

Ashmead, A.S. "The vegetarian question". In *Index-Lancet*, 33:359, 1910.

Badenoch, A. "Diet and stamina". In *Br. Med. J.*, 2:445, 668, 1952.

Badenoch, J. "The use of labelled B_{12} and gastric biopsy in investigation of anemia". In *Proc. R. Soc. Med.*, 47:426, 1954.

Banerjee, "Serum B_{12} in Vegetarians". In *Br. Med. J.*, 1 Oct., 1960.

Baptist, N.G. "Growth and amino acid intakes of a child on cereal, legume and vegetable diet". *Br. J. Nut.* 9:1955.

Barclay, R.W. "Organic Foods". In *J. Home Econ.* 64:2, 1972.

Barrow, J.G. "Prevalence of atherosclerotic complications in Trappist monks". In *Circulation*, 24:881, 1961.

_____. "Studies in Atherosclerosis (Trappists)". In *Ann. Intern. Med.*, 52:368, 1960.

Barskiy, B.I. "Effect of vegetarian diet on elimination of sterols from organisms". *Klin. Med.*, 18:69, 1940.

Bavetta, L.A. "Food Fads and Faddists". In *Am. J. Dig. Dis.*, 22:178, June, 1955.

Beeuwkes, A.M. "Food Faddism and the Consumer". In *Fed. Proc.*, 13:785, 1954.

Benedict, F.G. "The basal caloric output of vegetarians as compared with that of non-vegetarians of like weight and height". In *Proc. Nat. Acad. Sci.*, 1:1915.

_____. "The Metabolism of vegetarians compared with non-vegetarians of like weight and height". In *J. Biol. Chem.*, 20:263, 1915.

_____. "Metabolism of vegetarians as compared with non-vegetarians" *J. Biol. Chem.*, 20:231, 1915.

Berg, J.W. *Cancer Journal*, Dec., 1973.

Bernard, V.W. "Why people become the victims of Medical Quackery". In *Am. J. Pub. Health*, 55:1142, 1965.

Besant, Annie. *Vegetarianism in the Light of Theosophy.* Madras, India: Theosophical Publishing House, 1919.

Boitel, F. "Metabolism: Studies on older children on vegetarian diet". In *Arch. f. Kinderheilk,* 98:168, 1933.

Bonnejoy, E. "Le vegetarisme rationnel scientifique", 1889.

Booth, C.C. "Vitamin B_{12} deficiency due to defective diet". In *Lancet,* 1:727, 1956.

Bourne. "Dietary Vitamin B_{12} deficiency". In *Br. Med. J.,* 2:511, 1960.

Bronner, H. "Effect of diet on hydrogen iron concentration of bile". In *Clinical Observations,* Klin. Wochenschr., 12:1562, 1933.

Brown, P.T. "The dietary status of practising macrobiotics". In *Ecol. Food Nutr.,* Nov., 1975.

——. "The dietary status of 'New Vegetarians'". In *J. Am. Diet. Assoc.,* 67(5):455, Nov., 1975.

Bruch, H. "The allure of food cults and nutrition quackery". In *J. Am. Diet. Assoc.,* 57:316, 1970.

Burleigh, F.A. "The experience of a vegetarian". In *Phila. Polyclin.,* 6:11, 1897.

Buttner, J.L. *A fleshless diet: Vegetarianism as a rational dietary.* N.Y.: F.A. Stokes Co., 1910.

Calatayd, J.B. "Long term, low fat, low protein diets and their effect on normal Trappist subjects". In *Am. J. Clin. Nutr.,* 12:368, 1963.

Carlson, A.J. "Growth and longevity of rats fed vegetarian diets". In *J. Nutr.,* 34:81, Jul., 1947.

Carson, G. *Cornflake Crusade,* 1957.

Caspari, W. "Study of respiratory exchange of vegetarians". In *Arch. f.d. ges. Physiol.,* 109:473, 1905.

Cham. "The members of the Vegetarian Society". In *J. Hist. Med.* (Lithograph), 29:106, Jan., 1974.

Chang, C.Y. "Parathyroid hypertrophy and hypocalcemia in vegetarian rats". In *Chin. J. Physiol.,* 15:19, 1940.

_____. "Life span on vegetarian and omnivorous diets". In *Chin. J. Physiol.*, 16:229, 1941.

_____. "Effect of vegetarian diet on rate of respiration of rat organs". In *Chin. J. Physiol.*, 14:147, 1939.

Chapman, C.B. "The effect of rice-fruit diet on the composition of the body". In *New Eng. J. Med.*, 243:899, 1950.

Chen, J.S. "Effect of long-term vegetarian diet on serum lipid and lipoprotein levels in man". In *J. Formosan Med. Assoc.*, 65(2):65, 28 Feb., 1966.

Chen, T.T. "Cataract in Vegetarian rats". In *Chinese J. Physiol.*, 16:241, 1941.

_____. "Further observations". In *Chinese J. Physiol.*, 16:251, 1941.

Cherry, F.F., et al. "Cow versus soy formulas". In *Am. J. Dis. Child.*, 115:677-92, 1968.

Cheyne, G. "Essay on regimen."

Conner, P.M. "Nutritional vitamin B_{12} deficiency". In *Med. J. Australia*, 2:451, 1963.

Contet, E. "Les regimes vegetariens et la medecine". In *Arch. Gen. de Med.*, Paris, 1:135, 1907.

Cooke, R.T. "Megaloblastic anemia in a young vegetarian". In *Br. Med. J.*, 1:558, 1944.

Cornwall, E.E. "Case of Luigio Cornaro and how he balanced his diet". In *Med. J. and Record*, 126:309, 1927.

Cotes, J. "Possible effect of vegan diet upon lung function…in healthy women". In *J. Physiol.*, 209: suppl., July, 1970.

Crowther, J.S. "Sarcina ventriculi in human feces". *J. Med. Microbiol.*, 4(3):343, Aug., 1971.

DasGupta, C.R. "Vitamin B_{12} in nutritional macrocytic anemia". In *Br. Med. J.*, p. 645, 19 Sept., 1953.

Dastur, D.K. "Effect of vegetarianism and smoking on Vitamin B_{12}, thiocyanate and folate in blood of normal subjects". In *Br. Med. J.* 3(821):260, 29 July, 1972.

———. "Inter-relation between B-vitamins in B_{12} deficient neuro-myelopathy: A possible malabsorption-malnutrition syndrome". In *Am. J. Clin. Nut.*, 28(11):1255, Nov., 1975.

Davies, D. "A Shangri-la in Ecuador". In *New Sci.*, 57:236, 1973.

Dawber, Thomas. "Annual Discourse—Unproved Hypothesis". In *NEJM*: Aug. 31, 1978.

Dent, C.E. "Plasma 25-hydroxyvitamin-D levels during pregnancy in Caucasians and in vegetarian and non-vegetarian Asians". In *Lancet*, 2(7944): 1057, 29 Nov., 1975.

Deutsch, R.M. *The nuts among the berries: An expose of food fads.* N.Y.: Ballantine, 1961.

De Wijn, J. "Study of effects...vegetarian diet". In *Proc. Nutr. Soc.*, 13:14, 1954.

Dhopeshwarkar. "The effect of vegetarianism and antibiotics upon proteins and vitamin B_{12} in blood". *Br. J. Nut.*, 10:105, 1956.

Disler, P.B. "Effect of tea on iron absorption". In *Gut*, 16(3):193, Mar., 1975.

Domb, D.B. "The solution of sickness and disease with the plea for vegetarianism". In *Indianapolis Med. J.*, 16:381, 1913.

Donath, W. "Health, diet and vegetarianism". In *Nut. Abstr. and Rev.*, 23:892, 1953.

Donath, W.F. "Data on effects of diets free from animal proteins (Preliminary report)". In *Nederl. Tijdschr. Geneesk.*, 97:2118, 15 Aug., 1953.

Doyle, M.D. "Observations on nitrogen and energy balance in young men consuming vegetarian diet". In *Am. J. Cl. Nutr.*, 17:367, Dec., 1965.

Drasar. "The relation between diet and the gut microflora in man". In *Proc. Nutr. Soc.*, 32(2):49, Sept., 1973.

Druitt, A.F. "Health in relation to meatless diet". *Pub. Health*, 50:179, March, 1937.

Dwyer, J.T. "The 'New Vegetarians': Group affiliation and dietary strictures related to attitudes and life styles". In *J. Am. Diet. Assoc.*, 64:(4):376, Apr., 1974.

____. "The new vegetarians: The natural high?" In *J. Am. Diet. Assoc.*, 65(5):529, Nov., 1974.

____. "Vegetarianism in Drug Users". In *Lancet*, 2(739):1429, 25 Dec., 1971.

Eastwood, M. "Dietary fibre and serum lipids". In *Lancet*, 2(632): 1222, 6 Dec., 1969.

Ebstein, E. "Historical notes on vegetarianism". *Med. Life*, 31:469, 1924.

Edelstein, E. "Influence of addition of vegetables to the diet on metabolism of nitrogen minerals in children". In *Ztschr. F. Kinderheilk.*, 52:483, 1932.

____. "Vegetable diet in the feeding of children". In *Deutsch. Med. Wochenschr.*, 57:839, 1931.

Edmunds. "Questions suggested by vegetarianism with personal evidence from vegetarians". In *Proc. Med. Soc.*, 3:169, 1975.

Edwards, C. "Odd dietary practices of women". In *J. Am. Diet. Assoc.*, 30:976, Oct., 1954.

Eimer, K. "How far is it possible to affect acid base balance by vegetarian diet". In *Verh. d. Deutsch. Ges. f. Inn. Med.*, 43rd Congress, 1931.

____. "Protein metabolism during athletic training on uncooked vegetarian diet". In *Ztschr. f. d. Ges. Exp. Med.*, 81:703, 1932.

____. "Uncooked vegetarian diet and sports". In *Ztschr. f. Ernahrung*, 3:193, 1933.

____. "Vegetarian diet and heat regulation". In *Deutsch. Arch. f. Klin. Med.*, 173:314, 1932.

Ellis, F.R. "The health of vegans". In *Plant Foods in Hum. Nutr.* 2:93, 1971.

____. "Incidence of osteoporosis in vegetarians and omnivores". In *Am. J. Clin. Nutr.*, 25(6):555, June, 1972.

____. "Letter: Diet and colonic cancer". In *Br. Med. J.*, 2(917):505 1 June, 1974.

____. "The nutritional status of vegans and vegetarians". In *Proc Nutr. Soc.*, 26:205, 1967.

_____. "The treatment of dietary deficiency of vitamin B_{12} with vegetable protein foods". In _Nutr. Dieta._, 9:81, 1967.

_____. "Veganism: Clinical findings and investigations". In _Am. J. Clin. Nutr._, 23(3):249, Mar., 1970.

Erhard, D. "The new vegetarians: Part 1—Vegetarians and medical consequences". In _Nutr. Today_, 8:4, 1973.

_____. "The new vegetarians: Part 2—Zen Macrobiotics and other cults". In _Nutr. Today_, 9:20, Jan.-Feb., 1974.

_____. "A starved child of the new vegetarians". In _Nutr. Today_, 8:10, Nov.-Dec., 1973.

Fauvel, P. "A contribution to the study of vegetarianism". In _Mod. Med._, 16:8, 1907.

_____. "A vegetarian experiment". In _Mod. Med._, Battle Creek, Mich., 14:99, 1905.

Feeley, R.M. "Fat metabolism in pre-adolescent children on all-vegetable diets". In _J. Am. Diet. Assoc._, 47:396, 1965.

Ferrier, J. Todd. "On behalf of the creatures", 1930.

Fisher, I. "The effects of diet on endurance, New Haven, Connecticut". In _Yale Med. Jour._, 13:205, 1907.

Foote, R. "A dietary study of boys and girls on lacto-ovo-vegetarian diet". In _J. Am. Diet. Assoc._, 16:222, 1940.

Frank, L.J. "The meatless diet". In _Mod. Hosp._, 17:429, 1921.

Frankle, R.T. "Food zealotry and youth". In _Am. J. Pub. Health_, 64(1):11, Jan., 1974.

Friedman. "On vegetarianism". In _J. Am. Psychoanal. Assoc._ 23(2):396, 1975.

Gandhi. _Diet and Diet Reform_. Ahmedabad, India: Navajivan Publ. House, 1949.

Gandhi, M.K. _The Moral Basis of Vegetarianism_. Ahmedabad, India: Navajivan Publ. House, 1959.

Gassendi, P. _Collected works including his correspondence_. Lyons: Montmort, 1658.

Gauducheau, A. "Diet of modern man—evolution". In *Presse Med.*, 45:903, 16 June, 1937.

Gautier, A. "Le regime vegetarien". In *Rev. Scient.*, 1:65, 1904.

Gilson, E. "Historical notes on development of diet therapy". In *J. Am. Diet. Assoc.*, 23:761, Sept., 1947.

Giorgio, A. "Pseudo-Kayser Fleischer Rings". In *Arch. Intern. Med.* 113:817, June, 1964.

Gleeson, M.H. "Complications of dietary deficiency of vitamin B_{12} in young Caucasians". In *Postgrad. Med. J.*, 50(585):462, July, 1974.

Glyer, J. "Diet Healing: A case study in the sociology of health". In *J. Nutr. Educ.*, 4:163, 1972.

Gorman, J.C. "Calculations and analysis of fatty acids in vegetarian diets". In *J. Am. Diet. Assoc.*, 50(5):372, May, 1967.

Graham, S. *Science of human life.* Boston: Marsh, Capen, Lyon and Webb, 1858.

Green, J.D. "Megaloblastic anemia in a vegetarian taking oral contraceptives". In *South. Med. J.*, 68(2):249, Feb., 1975.

Groen, J. "Dietary deficiency as cause of macrocytic anemia". In *Am. J. of Med. Sc.*, 193:633, 1937.

____. "Influence of nutrition...Trappist monks". In *Am. J. Clin. Nutr.*, 10:456, 1962.

____. "The influence of nutrition and way of life...in Trappist and Benedictine monks". In *Ned. T. Geneesk.*, 105:222, 1961.

Groom-Napier, C.O. *Vegetarianism: A cure for intemperance.* London: William Tweedie, 1875.

Grosse-Brockhoff, F. "Behavior of nitrogen balance and blood proteins during vegetarian and lacto-vegetarian diet". *Deutsches Arch. Klin. Med.* 197:378, 1950.

Guggenheim, K. "Composition and nutritional value of diets consumed by strict vegetarians". In *Br. J. Nutr.*, 16:467, 1962.

Guinee, P. "E. coli with resistance factors in vegetarians, babies and nonvegetarians". In *Appl. Microb.*, 20(4):531, Oct. 1970.

Habs, H. "Metabolic investigation on vegetarians". In *Klin. Wochenschr.*, 11:715, 1932.

Haddon, J. "Vegetable vs. animal food". In *Arch. Roentg. Ray*, 10:7, 1905-6.

Haler, D. "Death after vegan diet". In *Lancet*, 2(560):170, 20 July, 1968.

Hall, A.A. "Some aspects of Vegetarianism". In *Harpers Mag.*, 123: 207, 1911.

Halsted, J.A. "Serum B_{12} concentration in dietary deficiency". In *Am. J. Clin. Nutr.*, 8:374, 1960.

Hamilton, J.B. "Life and times of Dr. Mussey". In *J. Am. Med. Assoc.*, 26:649, 1896.

Hardinge, M. "Nutritional, physical, and laboratory studies". In *J. Clin. Nut.*, 2(2):73, 1954.

———. "Dietary and serum levels of cholesterol". In *J. Clin. Nut.*, 2(2): 83, 1954.

———. "Dietary levels of fiber". In *J. Clin. Nut.*, 6(5):523, 1958.

———. "Dietary fatty acids and serum cholesterol levels". In *J. Clin. Nutr.*, 10:516, 1962.

———. "Proteins and essential amino acids". In *J. Am. Diet. Assoc.*, 48, 25, 1966.

———. "Historical background". In *J. Am. Assoc.*, 43:545, 1963.

———. "Scientific literature". In *J. Am. Assoc.*, 43:550, 1963.

———. "Adequate and inadequate". In *J. Am. Assoc.*, 45:537, 1964.

Harrison, R.J. "Vitamin B_{12} deficiency due to defective diet". In *Lancet*, 270:727, 1956.

Hart, E.B. "Growth on strictly vegetarian diets". In *Proc. Am. Soc. Biol. Chemists*, 1916, p.28.

Hegsted, D. "Protein requirements of adults". In *J. Lab. Clin. Med.*, 31:261, 1946.

____. "Lysine and Methionine supplements of all-vegetable diets for human adults". In *J. Nut.*, 56:555, 1955.

Heisler, A. "Sequels of exclusive fruit diet". In *Med. Welt*, 6:415, 19 Mar., 1932.

Hepner, G.W. "Altered bile acid metabolism in vegetarians". In *Am. J. Dig. Dis.*, 20(10):935, Oct., 1975.

Herschell, G. "Entirely lean meat diet (cannibals)". In *Lancet*, 2:950, 1889.

Hertzler, A. "Food guides in the U.S.: An historical review". In *J. Am. Diet. Assoc.*, 64(L):19, Jan., 1974.

Heupke, W. "Vegetarian diet". In *Ztschr. f. Ernahrung.*, 2:353, 1932.

Heussenstamm, F.K. "Teenage vegetarians: A study of motivation". A paper, 1971.

Higginbottom, M.C. et al. "A syndrome of methylmalonic aciduria—in a vitamin B_{12} deficient breast-fed infant of a strict vegetarian." In *New England Journal of Medicine*, Vol. 299, 1978, p. 317.

Hill, A.F. *Vegetarian essays*. Lond.: Ideal Publ. Unions, 1897.

Hill, C. "Foods and Fads". In *J.R. Soc. Arts.*, 100:181, 1952.

Hill, L. "Strict vegetarian diet". In *Br. Med. J.*, 2:417, 20 Aug., 1938.

Hill, M.J. "Diet and fecal flora". In *J. Path.*, 104:239, 1971.

____. "Fecal Steroid Composition and its relationships to cancer of the large bowel". In *J. Pathol.*, 104:129-139, 1971.

Himwich, W.A. "Lafayette B. Mendel and his scientific ancestry". In *J. Am. Diet. Assoc.*, 27:726, 1951.

Hindhede, M. "Blockade". In *J. Am. Med. Assoc.*, 72:1198, 1919.

____. "Effect of food restriction during the war on mortality in Copenhagen". In *J. Am. Med. Assoc.*, 74:381, 1920.

____. "Havebrug Skolonen 'Eden'". Nineteenth report, 1923.

____. "Meat diet as a cause of organic diseases". In *Med. Welt*, 3:537, 13 April, 1929.

Hines, J. "Megaloblastic anemia in adult vegetarians". In *Am. J. Clin. Nutr.*, 19:260, Oct. 1966.

Hoffbrand, A.V. "Blood and neoplastic disease: Megaloblastic anemia". In *Br. Med. J.*, 2(918):550, 8 June, 1974.

Holmes, J. "Cerebral manifestations of vitamin B_{12} deficiency". In *Br. Med. J.*, 2:1394, 1956.

Holmes, J.M. "Nutritional edema in a vegetarian". In *Br. Med. J.*, 1:620, 1944.

Hopkins, E.W. "The Buddhistic rule against eating meat". *J. Am. Oriental Soc.*, 27:455, 1906.

Hosmes-Gore, V. *These we have not loved.* 1942.

Huenemann, R.L. "Combating food misinformation and quackery". *J. Am. Diet. Assoc.*, 32:623, 1956.

Hughes. "Intakes of essential amino acids of children who were deriving most of their protein from bread and vegetables". In *Br. J. Nutr.*, 9:373, 1955.

Hunter, R. "Why Popeye took Spinach". In *Lancet*, 1(702): 10 Apr. 1971.

Jadhav, M. "Vitamin B_{12} deficiency in Indian infants". In *Lancet*, 2:903, 1962.

Jaffa, M.E. "Nutritional investigation among fruitarians and Chinese". In USDA, *Agric. Bull.*, No. 107, 1901.

Jagenburg, R. "Self-induced protein-calorie-malnutrition in a healthy adult male". In *Acta Med. Scand.*, 183(1):67, Jan.-Feb., 1968.

Jathar, V.S. "Serum B_{12} in Indian psychiatric patients". In *Br. J. Psych.*, 117:699, 1970.

____. "Vitamin B_{12} and Vegetarianism in India". In *Acta Haem.* (Basel), 53(2):90, 1975.

Jeffs, S. "Dietary deficiency and vitamin B_{12}". In *Br. Med. J.*, 2:732, 1960.

Jenkins, R.R. "Health implications of vegetarian diet". In *J. Am. Coll. Health Assoc.*, 24(2):68, Dec., 1975.

Jhatakia. "Profile of coronary artery disease in a vegetarian community". In *Ind. Heart. J.*, 25(2):94, Apr., 1973.

Johnston, C.M. "Nutrition and life style". In *J. Am. Diet. Assoc.*, 63(3):275, Sept., 1973.

Journals: *British Vegetarian, Children's Garden, Herald of the Golden Age, Vegetarian, Vegetarian Messenger, Vegetarian News, Ideal Publishing Union*, London, (reprints of early vegetarian literature approximately 1910).

Jukes, T.H. "Fact and fancy in nutrition and food science: Chemical residues in food". In *J. Am. Diet. Assoc.*, 59:203, 1971.

_____. "The organic food myth". In *J. Am. Med. Assoc.*, 230(2):276, 14 Oct., 1974.

Kamil, A. "How natural are those natural vitamins?" In *Nutr. Rev.*, 32:34, Supp., Jul., 1974.

Kark, R. "Tropical deterioration and nutrition: Clinical and biochemical observations on troops". In *Medicine*, 26:1, 1947.

Kaunitz, H. "Intestinal gases following mixed and vegetarian diets". In *Klin. Wochenschr.*, 15:1885, 1936.

Keith, M.H. "Is vegetarianism based on sound science?" In *Sciet. Am.*, 82:358, supp., 1916.

Kellogg, J.H. *The natural diet for man*. Battle Creek, Michigan Modern Med. Publ. Co., 1923.

_____. *Shall we slay to eat?* Battle Creek, Michigan: Good Health Publ Co., 1889.

Kempner, W. "Treatment of hypertensive vascular disease with ric diet". In *A.M.J. Med.*, 4:545-577, 1948.

Kern, K. "Importance of vegetarian diet for young children". I *Munch. Med. Wochenschr.*, 80:385, 1933.

Kern, R. A. "Diet as a factor in etiology of anemia". In *Ann. In Med.*, 5:729, 1931-32.

Kingsford, A. *The perfect way in diet*. London:Kegan, Paul, Trenc and Co., 1885.

Kirkeby, K. "Blood lipids, lipoprotein and protein in vegetarians". I *Acta Med. Scand.*, suppl. #443:1, 1966.

____. "The fatty acid composition in serum of Norwegian vegetarians". In *Acta Med. Scand.*, 183(1):143, Jan.-Feb., 1968.

Klewitz. "Vegetarian diet". In *Sitzungsber. Ges. Z. Beforderung d. Ges. Naturwissensch.*, 66:13, 1931.

Kodicek, E. "Vegetarian diet and nicotinic acid". In *Lancet*, 242:380, 1942.

Kuo-Hoa, L. "Nutritive value of vegetarian diets from an economic standpoint". In *Nat. Med. J.*, China, 17:200, Apr., 1931.

Lake, G.B. "Pros and cons of vegetarianism". In *Am. Med.*, 39:460, Oct. 1933.

Lambe, W. *Reports of the effects of a peculiar regime in scirrhous tumors and cancerous ulcers.* London: J. Mawman, 1809.

Lampkin, B.C. "Nutritional vitamin B_{12} deficiency in an infant". In *J. Ped.*, 75(6):1053, Dec., 1969.

Lane, C. "A brief practical essay on vegetable diet". 1847.

Lane, D.E. "Nutrition of children on vegetarian diet: Growth and allergy". In *Am. J. Dis. Child.*, 52:1397, Dec., 1936.

____. "Nutrition of twins on a vegetarian diet during pregnancy, nursing and infancy". In *Am. J. Dis. Child.*, 42:1384, 1931.

____. "Vegetarian diet vs mixed". In *Am. J. Phys. Therapy*, 11:16, Jun., 1934.

Layrisse, M. "Food iron absorption: A comparison of vegetable and animal foods". In *Blood*, 33(3):430, Mar., 1969.

Leaf, A. "Every day is a gift when you're over 100". In *Nat. Geog.* 143(1):93, 1973.

Ledbetter, R.B. "Severe megaloblastic anemia due to nutritional vitamin B_{12} deficiency". In *Acta Haematol.* 42:247, 1969.

Lee, K. "Geographic studies of atherosclerosis: Effect of vegetarian diet on lipids, ECG". In *Arch. Envir. Health*, Chicago, 4:4, Jan., 1962.

Lehninger, Albert L. *Biochemistry.* Worth Publishers, 1972.

Leitner, Z.A. "Fatal self-medication with retinol and carrot juice". In *Proc. Nutr. Soc.*, 34(2):44A, Sept., 1975.

Lemon, F.R. "Cancer of lung and mouth in Seventh Day Adventists". In *Cancer*, 17:489, Apr., 1964.

____. "Death from respiratory system disease among Seventh Day Adventist men". In *J. Am. Med. Assoc.*, 198:117, 1966.

Leverton, R.M. "Nutritional value of organically grown foods". In *J. Am. Diet. Assoc.*, 62:501, 1973.

Levinson, S.A. "The effect of a relief vegetable protein diet on normal human subjects'. In *J. Am. Diet. Assoc.*, 22:987, 1946.

Lieb, C.W. "Effects of an exclusive, long continued meat diet" In *J. Am. Med. Assoc.*, 87:25, 1926.

Lin, K.H. "Nutritive value of vegetarian diets from an economic standpoint". In *Nat. Med. J. China*, 17:200, 1931.

____. "Estrous rhythm of vegetarian and omnivorous rats". In *Chinese J. Physiol.*, 6:23, 1932.

____. "A study on the food consumption of omnivorous and vegetarian rats". In *Nat. Med. J. China*, 17:729, 1931.

Linnell, J.C. "Patterns of plasma cobalamin in controls and in vitamin B_{12} deficiency". In *J. Clin. Path.*, 22(5):545, Sept., 1969.

Lowenstein, F. "Epidemiological aspects of blood pressure and its relation to diet". In *Am. Heart J.*, 47:874, Jun., 1954.

Mack, P.B. "Comparison of meat and legumes: A seven-month study of 24 children". In *J. Am. Diet. Assoc.*, 23:588, July, 1947.

Majumder, S.K. "Vegetarianism: Fad, faith or fact". In *Am. Scientist*, 60(2):175, Mar.-Apr., 1972.

Malmros, H. "A statistical study of effect of wartime on atherosclerosis...". In *Acta Med. Scand.*, Suppl. #246:137, 1950.

Mann, G. "Vegetarianism and drug users". In *Lancet*, 1:381, 12 Feb., 1972.

Marsh, A.G. "Metabolic response of adolescent girls to lacto-ovo-vegetarian diet". In *J. Am. Diet. Assoc.*, 51(5):441, Nov., 1967.

Mauriac, P. "Green vegetable diet in treatment of diabetics under insulin: Advantages and dangers". In *Schweiz. Med. Wochenschr.*, 65:382, 1935.

Maynard, L.A. "Effect of fertilization on the nutritional value of foods". In *J. Am. Med. Assoc.*, 161:1478, 11 Aug., 1956.

Mayo, C.W. "Man and his diet: Man compared to carnivora and herbivora". In *Mouth Health Quart.*, 5:5, Jan.-Mar., 1936.

McBean, L.D. "Food faddism: A challenge to nutritionists". In *Am. J. Clin. Nutr.*, 27:1071, Oct., 1974.

McCance, R. "Old thoughts and new work on breads, white and brown". In *Lancet*, No. 6882:205, 1955.

McCollum, E.V. "The Vegetarian diet in light of our present knowledge of nutrition". In *Am. J. Physiol.*, 41:333, 1916.

McCullagh, E.P. "Study of diet, blood lipids and vascular disease in Trappist monks". In *New Eng. J. Med.*, 263:569, 1960.

McKenzie, J.C. "Profile on vegans". In *Plant Foods Human Nutr.*, 2:79, 1971.

____. "Social and economic implications of minority food habits". In *Proc. Ntr. Soc.*, 26:197, 1967.

Mehta. "Serum B_{12} and folic activity in lacto-vegetarian and non-vegetarian healthy adult Indians". In *Am. J. Clin. Nutr.*, 15: Aug., 1964.

Mendel, L.B. "Some historical aspects of vegetarianism". In *Pop. Sc. Month.*, 64:457, 1903-04.

Miles, H.E. *Economy in wartime or health without meat.* London: Methuen and Co., 1915.

Mirone, L. "Blood findings in men on a diet devoid of meat and low in animal protein". In *Science*, 3:16, June, 1950.

____. Nutrient intake and blood findings of men on a diet devoid of meat". In *Am. J. Clin. Nutr.*, July-Aug., 1954.

Misra, H.N. "Subacute combined degeneration of the spinal cord in a vegan". In *Postgrad. Med. J.*, 47(551):624, Sept., 1971.

Mollin, D.L. "The Serum Vitamin B_{12} Level: Its Assay and Significance". In *Clin. In Haem*, Vol. 5, No. 3, Oct., 1976, pp. 521-546.

Moncriff, B. "The philosophy of the stomach or an exclusively animal diet (without any vegetables or condiment whatever) is the most wholesome and fit for man" (illustrated by experiments upon himself). London: 1856.

Montheath, K. *Science in diet: A thesis on vegetarianism*. London: Chapman and Wilson, 1922.

Moore, W.E. "Fecal flora on changing to a vegetarian diet". In *J. Inf. Dis.*, 119:641, 1969.

Morgan, A.F. "Complete non-meat ration for dogs". In *North Am. Vet.*, 10:28, Nov., 1929.

Morgan, D. "Meatless in Norway". In *Ithaca J.*, 15 Nov., 1974, p. 10.

Muley, K. "Food in the east and in the west: Comparative studies". In *Ztschr. F. Ernahrung*, 1:361, 1931.

Nagy, M. "Natural vs synthetic vitamins". In *J. Am. Med. Assoc.*, 225:73, 1973.

_____. "Teenage vegan". In *J. Am. Med. Assoc.*, 211:306, 1970.

Narayanan, M. "Reciprocal elevation in serum levels ot vitamin B_{12} in patients with nutritional macrocytic anemia". In *Ind. J. Med. Sc.*, 11:163, 1957.

Newman, F.W. *Essays on diet*. 1883.

Ohlson, M.A. "Dietary patterns and effect on nutrient intake". In *World Ref. Nutr. Diet.*, 10:13, 1969.

Oldham, H. "Effect of caloric intake on nitrogen utilization during pregnancy". In *J. Am. Diet. Assoc.*, 27:847, 1951.

Oser, W. "Vegetarian diet in infant feedings". In *Schweiz. Med. Wochenschur.*, 62:91, 1932.

Paget, Lady W. "Vegetable diet". In *Pop. Sc. Month.*, 44:94, 1893-4

Pezold, F.A. "Position of vegetarian diet in modern dietetics". In *Deutsches Med. J.*, 5:378, 9 June, 1954.

Pfeffer, K.H. "The sociology of nutrition, malnutrition and hunger in developing countries". In VIII Symposium of the Swedish Nutrition Foundation: *Food Cultism and Nutrition Quckery,* Stockholm, Almquist and Wiksells, 1972, edited by G. Blix, p.30.

Phillips, R.M. In *Cancer Research*, Nov., 1975.

Pillai, P.W. "Is man adapted naturally to eat vegetables alone?" *Indian Med. Rec.*, 9:120, 1895.

Pollycove, M. "Pernicious anemia due to dietary deficiency of vitamin B_{12}". In *New Eng. Med. J.*, 255:164, 1956.

Pomare, E.W. "Change in bile sale metabolism by dietary fibre". In *Br. Med. J.*, 4:262, 1973.

Potterton, D. "Growing up a vegetarian". In *Nursing Times*, March 30, 1978.

Prakash. "Cysticercosis with Taeniasis in a vegetarian". In *J. Trop. Med. and Hygiene*, April, 1965.

Prout, C. "Dietary restriction: The new nirvana". In *Trans. Am. Clin. Climatol. Assoc.*, 83:219, 1972.

Raab, W. "Circulatory organs in vegetarians and in alcoholics...". In *Ztschr. f. Klin. Med.*, 130:505, 1936.

Ramachandran, M. "Nutritional value of vegetable proteins, Part III: Biosynthesis of vitamin B_{12} and utilization in rats on vegetable protein diets". In *Ind. J. Med. Res.*, 48:243, Mar., 1960.

Raper, N.R. "Vegetarian Diets". In *Nutr. Rev.*, 32(0): Suppl. 1:29, July, 1974.

Register, U.D. "Nitrogen balance in humans on various diets". In *Am. J. Clin. Nutr.*, 20(7):753, July, 1967.

———. "The vegetarian diet, Scientific and practical considerations". *J. Am. Diet. Assoc.*, 62(3):253, Mar., 1973.

Reuben, David. *Everything you always wanted to know about nutrition.* Schuster, 1978.

Rietschel, H. "Disseminated sclerosis: Raw vegetable food in disseminated sclerosis". In *Ernahrung*, 1:727, 1936.

Riley, C.J. "Unusual case of subacute combined degeneration of the spinal cord". In *Br. Med. J.*, 2:566, 1966.

Robson, J.R. "Zen macrobiotic diet". In *Lancet*, 1(815):1327, 9 June, 1973.

Robson, J.R.K. "Zen macrobiotic diet: Problems in infancy". In *Pediatrics*, 53:326, 1974.

Roels, O.A. "Serum lipids and diet: Comparison of three groups". In *J. Nutr.*, 79:211, 1963.

Rose, M.S. "Growth, reproduction and lactation on diets with different proportions of cereals and vegetables". In *J. Biol. Chem.*, 78: 535, July, 1928.

Rosebury, T. "Zen diets". In *J. Am. Med. Assoc.*, 218:1703, 1971.

Rudd, G.L. *Why kill for food.* 1956.

Sacks, F.M. "Plasma lipids and lipoproteins in vegetarians and controls". In *New Eng. J. Med.*, 292(22):1148, 29 May, 1975.

____. "Blood pressure in vegetarians". In *Am. J. Epid.*, 110(5):390, Nov., 1974.

Sahasrabudhe, N.S. "Radiologic study of GIT in vegetarians". In *Antiseptic*, 35:1, Jan., 1938.

Saille, F. "Influence of vegetable food on blood pressure". In *Med. Clin.*, 26:929, 1930.

Salt, H.S. "The humanities of diet". In *Fortnightly Rev.*, London, 9:426, 1896.

____. "A plea for vegetarianism and other essays". Manchester: 1886.

Sanborn, A.G. "Fecal flora of adults: Relation to effects of various diets". In *J. Inf. Dis.*, 48:541, June, 1931.

Satoskar. "Serum protein...in lacto...and non-vegetarians". In *Ind. J. Med. Res.*, 49:887, 1961.

Satyanarayana, N. "Plasma vitamin B_{12} levels in vegetarians". In *Ind. J. Med. Res.*, 51:380, Mar., 1963.

Schenck, W.L. "Letter on Dr. Mussey". In *J.A.M.A.*, 26:1236, 1896

Schloesser, L.L. "Vitamin B$_{12}$ absorption studies in a vegetarian with megaloblastic anemia". In *Am. J. Clin. Nutr.*, 12:70, 1963.

Schultzer, P. "Calcium and phosphorus metabolism in patients with osteomalacia, who had been vegetarian for 21 years". In *Am. J. Med. Sc.*, 186:532, Oct., 1933.

Scott, R. "Effect of diet on serum lipid metabolism". In *Am. J. Clin. Nutr.*, 13:82, 1963.

Scrimshaw, N.S. "All-vegetable protein mixtures for humans". In *Am. J. Clin. Nutr.*, 9:196, 1961.

____. "Vegetable protein mixtures for human consumption". In *Fed. Proc.*, 20: Suppl. 7:80, 1961.

Sebrell, W.H. "Food faddism and public health". In *Fed. Proc.*, 13:780, 1954.

Sena, B. *Beloved Master*. Franklin, N.H.: Sant Bani Press, 1970, p. 4.

Sheft, B.B. "Amino acid intakes and excretions during pregnancy". In *J. Am. Diet. Assoc.*, 28:313, 1952.

Shelley, P. *Vindication of natural diet.* 1813.

Sherlock, P. "Scurvy produced by a Zen macrobiotic diet". In *J.A.M.A.*, 199:794, 1967.

Shimoda. "Nutrition and lifestyle: II. Observations of a nutritionist in a free clinic". In *J. Am. Diet. Assoc.*, 63(3):273, Sept., 1973.

Shun, D.J. "Nutritional megaloblastic anemia in a vegan". In *N.Y. State J. Med.*, 72(23):2893, 1 Dec., 1972.

Silverberg. "Diet and life span". In *Physiol. Rev.*, 35:347, Apr., 1955.

Simoons, F.J. *Eat not this flesh: Food avoidances in old world.* Madison, Wisconsin: Univ. of Wis. Press, 1961.

Singh, B. "Nutritional macrocytic anemia amongst vegetarians in forward areas in Middle East campaign". In *Ind. Med. Gaz.*, 79L 531, Nov., 1944.

Singh, Kirpal. *The spiritual aspect of the vegetarian diet.* Franklin, N.H.: Sant Bani Press, 1970.

Sipple, H.L. "Food fads and fancies: A health problem". In *J. Agr. Food Chem.*, 2:352, 1954.

Slonaker, J.R. "The effect of omnivorous and vegetarian diets on reproduction in the albino rat". In *Science*, 47:223, 1918.

_____. *Effect of strict vegetarian diet on spontaneous activity and rate of growth and longevity of albino rat.* Stanford, California: Stanford Univ. Publ., 1912.

Smith, *Fruits and farinacea the proper food for man.*

Smith, A.D.M. "Veganism: A clinical survey with observations on B$_{12}$ metabolism". In *Br. Med. J.*, 16 June, 1962.

Smyth, J.C. *The work of the late William Stark, M.D.* London: J. Johnson, #72, St. Paul's Churchyard, 1788.

Sokolou, R.A. "A meat-eating 230-lb. M.D.: Now 175 lbs. vegetarian". In *The New York Times*, 38:12 Aug., 1971.

Spiro, H.M. "The rough and the smooth". In *New Eng. J. Med.*, 293(2):83, 10 July, 1975.

Stare. "Protein: Its role". In *J.A.M.A.*, 127:985, 1945.

Stare, F.J. "Health foods: Definition and nutritional value". In *J. Nutr. Ed.*, 4:94, 1972.

Stark, W. *The works of the late William Stark.* London: J. Johnson, 1788.

Steiner, P. "Necropsies on Okinawans". In *Arch. Path.*, 42:359, 1946.

Stewart, J.S. "Response of dietary vitamin B$_{12}$ deficiency to physiological oral doses of cyanocobalamin". In *Lancet*, 2(672):542, 12 Sept., 1970.

Strom, A. "Mortality from circulation disease in Norway, 1940-45". In *Lancet*, 260:126, 1951.

Stroupe, H.E. *The vegetarian.* Garden City, N.Y.: Country Life Press, 1916.

Stroupe, H.L. "The vegetarian". In *Jamaica*, N.Y., 1:187, 1916.

Subrahmanyan, V. "Metabolism of Nitrogen, Calcium, Phosphorous, in human adults on poor vegetarian diet containing ragi". In *Br. J. Nutr.*, 9:350, 1955.

Sullivan, L.W. "Studies on minimum daily requirements for vitamin B$_{12}$". In *New Eng. J. Med.*, 272:340, 1965.

Sutnick, M. "Vegetarian diets". In *Primary Care*, 2:#2, June, 1975.

Swan, J.M. "A study of the metabolism of a vegetarian". In *Am. J. Med. Sc.*, 129:1059, 1905.

Schweitzer, Albert. *Reverence for Life*. Philosophical Library, 1965.

Tang, P.S. "Notes on Nutrition of Chinese including physiological aspects of vegetarian diet". In *Biochem. Bull.*, #50, 52, 56, 58, 59, 60, 1945-1946.

Tang, Y. "The effect of a vegetarian diet on the learning ability of albino rats". *Contr. Nat. Res. Inst. Psychol.*, 1:1, 1932.

Taylor. "The meat ration and blood levels". In *Br. Med. J.*, #4596, 219, 1949.

Taylor, A.E. "Is vegetarianism capable of worldwide application?" In *Pop. Sc. Month.*, 79, 587, 1911.

Taylor, G. "Nutritional macrocytic anemia and the animal protein of diet". In *Br. Med. J.*, 1:800, 1945.

Todhunter, E.N. "Food habits, food fadism and nutrition". In *World Rev. Nutr. Diet.*, 16:286, 1973.

Treaster, J.B. "Yale versus those mushy vegetables". In *The New York Times*, 15 Nov., 1971.

Treber, G.J. *Why kill to eat.* W.Y. Source Pub., 1972.

Trowell, H. "Dietary fibre and CAD". In *Rev. Eur. Etud. Clin. Biol.*, 17(4):345, Apr., 1972.

Vegetarian Organizations: International Vegetarian Union, Vegan Society, Vegetarian Federal Union, 1889 and Vegetarian Society London.

Verjaal, A. "Combined degeneration of spinal cord due to deficient vitamin B$_{12}$". In *J. Neurol. Neurosurg. and Psych.*, 30:464, 1964.

Vy. "Nutritional value of a vegetarian diet". In *Am. J. Clin. Nutr.*, 25(7):647, July, 1972.

Wadia, N.H. "Role of vegetarianism, smoking and hydroxocobalamin in optic neuritis". In *Br. Med. J.*, 3(821):264, 29 July, 1972.

Wakham, G. "The basal metabolic rates of vegetarians". In *J. Biol. Chem.*, 97:155, 1932.

Walden, R.J. "Effect of environment on serum cholesterol, triglyceride distribution among Seventh-Day Adventists". In *Am. J. Med.*, 36:269, Feb., 1964.

Walker, A.R. "Sugar intake and CAD". In *Atherosclerosis*, 14(2): 137, Sept.-Oct., 1971.

Wan, S. "Chemical composition of bones of vegetarian and omnivorous rats". In *Chin. J. Physiol.*, 7:23, 15 Mar., 1933.

___. "Growth of vegetarian rats on omnivorous diet". In *Chin. J. Physiol.*, 5:71, 1931.

___. "Value of vegetarian diets for maintenance". In *Chin. J. Physiol.*, 6:251, 15 Aug., 1932.

Warren, E. "Vegetarian Protein Foods". In *Food Tech.*, 20:39-40, 1966.

West, E.D. "EEG in veganism, vegetarianism, and vitamin B_{12} deficiency, and in controls". In *J. Neurol. Neurosurg. and Psych.*, 29:391, 7 Oct., 1966.

___. "The psychological health of vegans of other groups". In *Plant Foods Hum. Nutr.*, 2:147, 1972.

___. "Diet and serum cholesterol levels: A comparison between vegetarian and non-vegetarian Seventh-Day Adventists". In *Am. J. Clin. Nutr.*, 21(8):853, Aug., 1968.

White, H.S. "The organic foods movement: What it is and what the food industry should do about it". In *Food Technology*, 26:29, Apr., 1972.

Widdowson, E.M. "Vitamin C in vegetarian children". In *Spec. Rep. Ser. Med. Res. Coun.*, London, #257, 1947.

Williams, E.R. "Making vegetarian diets nutritious". In *Am. J. Nurs.*, 75(12)2168, Dec., 1975.

Williams, H. *The ethics of diet.* 1883.

Wilson, F. *Food for the golden age.* 1954.

Wilson, J. "Metabolic relation between cyanide...vitamin B_{12} in smokers and non-smokers". In *Clin. Sci.*, 31:1, 1966.

Winawer, S.J. "Gastric and hematologic abnormalities in a vegan with nutritional vitamin B_{12} deficiency". In *Gastroent.*, 53(1): 130, July, 1967.

Wishart, G.M. "The efficiency and performance of a vegetarian racing cyclist under different diet conditions". In *J. Physiol.*, 82:189, 1934.

Wokes, F. "Human dietary deficiency of vitamin B_{12}". In *Voeding*, 16:590, 1955.

Wolnak, B. "Health foods: Natural, basic and organic". In *Food Drug. Cosmet. Law J.*, 27:453, 1972.

Wokes, F. "Anemia and B_{12} dietary deficiency". In *Proc. Nutr. Soc.*, 15:134, 1956.

____. "Direct use of plant materials by man". In *Br. J. Nutr.*, 6:118, 1952.

____. "Human dietary deficiency of vitamin B_{12}". In *Am. J. Clin. Nutr.*, 3:375, 1955.

____. *Studies of vegetarian children: Food, the deciding factor.* London: Allen Lane, 1941.

____. "Tobacco amblyopia". In *Lancet,* 2:526, 6 Sept., 1958.

Wolff, R.J. "Who eats for health". In *Am. J. Clin. Nutr.*, 26:438, 1973.

Wu, H. "Growth and reproduction of rats on vegetarian diets". In *Chin. J. Physiol.*, 3:157, 1929.

Wynder, E.L. "Calcium and CAD among Seventh-Day Adventists". In *Cancer,* 12:1016, 1959.

Yano, M. "The synthesis of vitamins by intestinal bacteria and the effect of cellulose, IV. Synthesis of vitamin B_6". In *J. Vitamin*, Osaka, Japan, 2(3):209, 10 Sept., 1956.

Youmans, J. "Surveys of nutrition of populations". In *Am. J. Public Health*, 33:955, 1943.

Yukawa, G. "The absolute vegetarian diet of Japanese Bonzes". In *Arch. Verdauungskr.*, 15:471, 1909.

Zolber, K. "Producing meals without meat". In *Hospitals*, 49(12): 811, 16 June, 1975.

Editorials and Miscellaneous

"Vegetarian diets". In *J. Am. Diet. Assoc.*, 65(2):121, Aug., 1974.

"Position paper on food and nutritional misinformation on selected topics". In *J. Am. Diet. Assoc.*, 66(3):277, Mar., 1975.

"Vegetarian diets". In *Am. J. Clin. Nutr.*, 27(10):1095, Oct., 1974.

"Fruits, vegetables and nuts". In *J.A.M.A.*, 108:1359, 17 Apr., 1937.

"Zen macrobiotics". In *J.A.M.A.*, 218:397, 1971.

"Animal versus vegetable protein". In *J.A.M.A.*, 105:438, 1935.

"Can a vegetarian be well-nourished?" In *J.A.M.A.*, 233(8):898, 25 Aug., 1975.

"Vegetarian diets for children". In *Br. Med. J.*, Apr., 1956.

"Food revisionists". In *Br. Med. J.*, 2(915):345, 18 May, 1974.

"Some thoughts on vegetarianism". In *Dietet. and Hyg. Gaz.*, 10: 237, 1894.

"Possible effect of vegan diet on lung function...". In *J. Physiol.*, 209, Suppl., Apr., 1970.

"Vegetarian diet". In *Med. Lett.*, 15(7):30, 30 Mar., 1973.

"Zen macrobiotic diet hazard, Passaic Grand Jury". In *Public Health News*, New Jersey State Dept. of Health, 132, June, 1966.